Marie-Claude PERRIN
Bernadette RIGAL-CELLARD

The Complete Stories

Flannery O'Connor

CNED

ARMAND COLIN

Conception de couverture : Jérôme Lo Monaco

ISBN : 2-200-26802-5

Table des matières

Première partie (Part I)

par Bernadette Rigal-Cellard

Seconde partie

par Marie-Claude Perrin-Chenour

Part I

This first part mostly deals with the religious orientation of the stories collected under the title *A Good Man Is Hard to Find* and explains the fundamental elements of the Christian doctrine Flannery O'Connor staged in her fiction because they are probably the most difficult to perceive. Non-religious people should not "despair": in spite of their religious intent, her stories can be appreciated by everyone for her debunking of self-righteous people is always burlesque and most pleasing to read.

Bernadette Rigal-Cellard

Introduction

Flannery O'Connor's life and work

Flannery O'Connor (1925-1964) was born in Savannah, Georgia. She studied in Georgia and in Iowa. Her master's thesis contained some of the short stories she would publish later. In 1950 she was diagnosed with lupus, an incurable disease that had already killed her father. The disease was treated with an experimental drug, derived from cortisone, but it weakened her bones and she had to walk with a cane and then with crutches. In 1951, she moved in with her mother on her farm, Andalusia, near Milledgeville, Georgia, a small country town rather different from the sophisticated cities she had lived in before. Her father had been the mayor of that town. She raised peacocks and in the morning she wrote fiction and many essays. Her life was restricted to the farm and to visits to universities for lectures. She thus lived her adult life alone with a fairly domineering mother, as she did not want to marry and have children for fear of transmitting them her hereditary fatal disease. Her fiction, deeply grounded in "real life" displays many young children or teenagers who have to bear their unpleasant widowed mothers (Josephine Hendin analyses such relations in the chapter "The enduring conflict" of *The World of Flannery O'Connor,* 1970)

Her major characteristic was her overpowering Catholic faith. To her the mystery of the Christian God and of His grace was all encompassing, and as an artist she devoted her art to spreading the good news to her reticent readers. She as a person looms large over her work: when she did not write fiction, she wrote letters or essays, or gave lectures dealing with her faith, with the design of her work, and she constantly prods her audience in a specific direction. Thus we can throw a light on her fictional texts by drawing from her other writings. Cleanth Brooks said in the memorial issue of *Esprit*: "In her instance I find it hard to separate the person from the artist." (*in* Friedman, 3)

Altogether she published two novels and twenty-six short stories. She began by publishing short stories in magazines. Her first book was a novel, *Wise Blood* (1952). It is the weird story of Hazel Motes who is an itinerant preacher modeled after Southern evangelists, but he is an agnostic who decides to found the "Church Without Christ". In itself this is extremely humorous, yet Motes has no sense of humor whatsoever, only a sense for the tragic, which he obviously misplaces. His journeys lead him to encounter ordinary people who disgust him. He finally blinds himself by pouring lime into his eyes because he believes in the metaphor according to which the blind are supposed to be able to see through the meaning of life.

Hazel Motes ends up beaten to death by two policemen who find him in a ditch. The mark of redemption must be seen in the pin point of light that his landlady, staring (with her eyes closed) into his blind eyes, feels he has become: "she saw him moving farther and farther away, farther and farther into the darkness until he was the pin point of light." This pin point of light had earlier been referred to as the star over Bethlehem. The central figure Hazel thinks he is escaping from, whereas he is constantly searching for it, is of course Christ. And his refusal to accept him, probably because he has grown tired of all the sermons he hears everywhere around him, is commuted in the end into an intimate fusion with Christ. In the author's note to the 1962 edition of the novel, the author called him "a Christian *malgré lui*".

The book was not understood immediately and was criticized because many saw it as a satire of Southern preachers and felt that Flannery O'Connor, as a Catholic, had no right to make fun of the faith of other people. It was only later that her perspective received more serious critical attention, thanks, to a great extent, to her own explanations.

The collection of short stories *A Good Man is Hard to Find* (GM) was published in 1955. Her second novel, *The Violent Bear it Away* (1960) tells the story of a young boy, Tarwater, who believes he is a prophet. He first rebels against the fanatic religion of the old uncle who raises him but he then accepts it and turns into one of its preachers. After drowning a child, to save him, or his family, he believes he has become a new Christ, at one point performing the miracle of the multiplication of bread loaves, and then Moses to whom the burning bush commands "GO WARN THE CHILDREN OF GOD OF THE TERRIBLE SPEED OF MERCY". The novel ends on his setting fire to his family farm and his resolute departure towards "the dark city, where the children of God lay sleeping."

Her second collection of short stories, *Everything That Rises Must Converge* was published after her death, in 1965. Her numerous essays, reviews and letters were published posthumously as well.

1

The religious essence of her works

Flannery O'Connor read intensively: the Bible, the writings of the Fathers of the Church and of various saints, mystics and theologians — Catholic and Protestant alike. Not unlike her fanatic Protestant preachers, she was fascinated by the prophets of the Old Testament and also, but unlike Protestants, by the many saints of the Catholic pantheon. She cannot be said to be very tolerant, and indeed she often borrowed the chastening rods of the Old Testament prophets revered by the Evangelists.

She wrought her stories very tightly, so as to put centuries of theological thought in a nutshell. In some circles now, she is even considered as a theologian herself. This chapter summarizes some of the Christian tenets that structure her fiction.

Christianity differs from other Biblical religions in its emphasis on the person of Christ and His function in our life.

The point of departure of the Christian epic that reverberates in O'Connor's fiction is the interpretation of **Evil**. Most cultures and spiritual systems address this basic problem since evil, suffering and violent death, are omnipresent in the world. To the Christians, evil is the consequence of sins, man's wrong actions understood as an offense to God. The first portentous sin is that of Adam and Eve who disobeyed God in their desire to reach knowledge. This **Original Sin** is transmitted from generation to generation, each individual carrying it in his/her "genes". It can only be washed away through the sacrament of **Baptism**, the cleansing of the soul, and through Redemption. The soul becomes at this point ready to meet God.

Catholicism teaches the freedom of each soul to choose between good and evil. The theory of **free will** has evolved over the centuries and is not shared by all Christians, though. If one is punished for choosing the wrong side, free will maybe an empty concept and theologians have argued intensely about this point. Flannery O'Connor's characters are free to choose, and they are not so much punished in the end as placed in front of the Truth: God's mystery.

The Old Testament centers on the **Covenant** between God and His people, the need for the people to obey the **Commandments** and the promise of a **Messiah** who would come and reverse the order of things. The New Testament, or **New Covenant**, reveals that, seeing the weakness of His children, God sent His true Son, the Messiah, to show them the right path, and to offer Himself as the ultimate sacrifice through which evil would be vanquished. This is the **Incarnation**. God becomes actually present in His **Creation** (what is enumerated in the Book of Genesis), transcendence (what is beyond our senses) is made immanent (present in the world): the transcendent God **manifests** Himself. For the Catholics such an act proves the essential goodness of Creation.

For groups such as the Manicheans (the followers of Mani who lived in Persia around 210-275), so famous now because of a wrong use of their name, God was so perfect that He could not have created a world of suffering and death, and therefore the creation was the work of the Devil, and the world of God was only in the Heavens. The created world (the earth, animals, men…) was to be abandoned and only the spiritual world to be sought for and contemplated. It is from such a radical separation between the two planes, that of the good (celestial world) and that of the bad (terrestrial world), that their name was taken to mean "dualism", which is however not quite adequate since dualism implies the double nature of things, each being both evil *and* good.

For several Protestant groups, Incarnation does not have the same force as in Catholicism and for them Creation is not necessarily good. Flannery O'Connor often declared that the phenomenon of Incarnation, totally mysterious but not to be questioned, was the revolutionary event that had transformed human fate.

Now, through His Incarnation as a man, Christ had to experience physical death, all men being doomed to die. Yet, since He is God, He is by essence immortal, and since human beings share in His essence (for He became one of them), they too are meant to be immortal. However, in order to reach this stage, they must be rid of their evil proclivity, and they cannot do so on their own. This was performed through the sacrifice of Christ, the **Crucifixion**, for it redeemed all sins, past, present and future. This is the mystery of redemption. It is a symbolical transfer.

The term **Redemption** comes from the Latin *redemptio*, to buy back. It is an act of redeeming, of deliverance from evil, sin and death. "It is the purchase of God's favor by the death and suffering of Christ; the ransom of deliverance of sinners from the bondage of sin and the penalties of God's violated law." (Webster Dictionary). It is also called the **Atonement**.

Redemption is an act stemming from the generosity of God, **Grace**. Within Christianity there are several interpretations as to the generality of this redemption and to the availability of Grace. Some groups do not consider that everyone can be redeemed by the sacrifice of Christ, and that one must deserve such generosity, either through faith, or good works, etc. Some say good works are of no avail, since one cannot decide how God will dispense His Grace. Only if God wants you to be saved, will you be saved (predestination). Some say it is enough to have Faith in the Grace of God. For the Catholics, Redemption is universal. Anybody can be therefore saved for all eternity. The only condition is to be conscious of one's failure, or one's mortal nature, and one must accept such a gift, the gift of the all-encompassing Grace of God. The stories of Flannery O'Connor hinge on this.

How does the actual act of Redemption operate? For a Catholic, this action can be immediate, with sins immediately forgiven, in confession with a priest or directly with God. Flannery O'Connor does not explain exactly what takes place at that point, but she shows that at the end of each story something positive has happened, through a specific description of the sun for example, or of light, or fire... These elements symbolize the power and love of God. In the end then the protagonists come to accept such power and they understand that their pride was misplaced and ridiculous.

Redemption accomplishes the **Justification** of the sinners, that is to say their salvation from evil through Grace, and not simply thanks to their own merit through good works or simple obedience to the Commandments. It is a term often heard in the mouths of American Evangelist preachers and in O'Connor as well.

The term comes from justice, originally from the Greek *dikaiosunè*, then translated into Latin *justificatio*. For the Greeks, the "just man" was the one who accomplished the virtuous acts necessary to the community. Yet in the Old Testament, the notion of justice is different: justice is not the appreciation of one self, or of the self of others, but the relation between man and the one who judges him, and that can only be God. The Just is no longer a virtuous man, nor a man transformed through a ritual of initiation, but man confronted with an accuser (the devil) and with his judge (God). Jesus manifests the sentence of God over mankind: nobody can justify him/herself, and one can only be justified through **Faith**, and the operation of Grace that cannot be ordered of course by men. (André Dumas, in *Dictionnaire de la Théologie chrétienne*).

The **Eucharist** is the specific ritual through which Faith and Grace are subsumed. The word comes from the Greek for thankfulness, gratitude, from *charis*, favor, grace. It is a paramount sacrament that reenacts the Last Supper of Christ through the consecration of the bread and wine that transmutes them into the actual body of Christ. This is called **Transubstantiation**. Once the priest has performed this, the **Elevation** takes place: the priest elevates the holy Host, which has thus become the Body of Christ, in a repetition of Christ's sacrifice offered to God, for the redemption of the worshippers and of the multitude of men. The believers are then called to share in the sacrifice, through Holy **Communion**, the eating of the Body of Christ. "A Temple of the Holy Ghost" ends on the powerful ritual of the Elevation: first the priest performs it in the chapel of the convent, and then God performs it at large in His Creation, through the red sun over the trees.

Catholicism centers its ritual, the mass, around the Eucharist. It offers the communion everyday and believers must take it at least once a year, during the Easter period, but preferably very regularly. They used to be obliged to have confessed their sins during Confession and to have fasted for a certain period of time (twelve hours at least) before partaking of the communion. The requirements have considerably been lowered, and one hour of fasting is now enough.

The Eucharist is not such a sacrament for the Protestants and the Churches that derive from Calvinism only offer Communion once or twice a year to their members. Furthermore only Catholicism teaches Transubstantiation, the other groups seeing the Eucharist as purely symbolical, which is less forceful. The Eucharist is performed notably at the end of "The Displaced Person", in a very subtle way as if to prove to the critics of the Church that Catholic rituals are not just pomp and circumstance, but very simple acts of interaction between man and his Maker.

Flannery O'Connor's stories are therefore models her readers must decipher so as to accept the sacrifice of Christ, to have faith, which then will change their lives radically. In fact this is all she really wanted to say: "It seems to me that all good stories are about **conversion**, about a character's changing [...]. The action of grace changes a character." (Letter, 1958, printed in *The Habit of Being*, ed. S. Fitzgerald. New York: Farrar and Strauss, 1979) She often refers to this act of conversion as a **vision**, a mysterious operation that transforms reality.

We may find this fascination strange because we are no longer accustomed to religious fiction in our country, but a few decades ago many of our best writers were also profoundly concerned with the relationships man entertained with the sacred and the problem of Good and Evil (see Gide, Mauriac, Bernanos, etc.).

We shall see how her fiction bears on the tension between the forces of secularity (the world of business, consumerism, see for example the role of cars, tractors, coca-cola, etc., in her stories) and the opposite forces of the sacred, of spirituality. She shows how the sacred invades our profane world through acts of violence that she turns into acts of redemption. For her "the dividing line between the prophetic and the demonic, the sacred and the profane, is often imperceptible, and her fictions both figure and transgress that line." (Patrick O'Donnell *in* Benét's, 799)

Even if one does not share Flannery O'Connor's preoccupation with the divine and redemption, one can still appreciate her stories for they draw upon a universal belief in the need for morality in everyday life and social encounters, in the power of spiritual or intellectual transformation of human beings when faced with the unknown and their own material limitations. In this respect, she allows her readers to experience the power of art to redeem us from the base level of instinctual and material life, and to transport us to another plane of human communication and understanding.

2

Narrative techniques

Even though she seemed to have preferred to write novels, her short stories are true gems. What she aims at (in particular showing the limitations and misplaced pride of people) is perfectly conveyed through these short cruel prose cartoons.

Showing or telling? Focalization

Flannery O'Connor never intervenes directly in her narrative to address the reader or point things at him/her. She shows how events develop and how they transform people from the inside out or the outside in, and how they get a better glimpse at life. These moments are usually at the very end of the stories, but their moral significance is never explicit. The reader must decipher the message by him/herself. We will return to this under the heading "Fables, allegories, parables".

The narrative technique adopted by Flannery O'Connor is not particularly original or experimental. She follows a rather traditional chronological plot line, without the fragmentation of time sequences. She associates them in a linear way and fuses time and eternity at the climax of the stories. She was not interested in the stream of consciousness technique fashionable in modernist fiction. She said she was bored with experimental fiction and felt very traditional (*in* Friedman 10). She admired François Mauriac for his Jansenism, or austere Catholicism and also for his classical narratives.

Focalization. She admitted having problems with the point-of-view (focalization) and her narrators seldom appear to be different from the author. She constantly uses third person narratives. Most often, the narrative voice shifts from one narrator to another, usually from the inner voice of the protagonists to that of an outside narrator, or to that of the author. Yet, even though Flannery O'Connor kept saying that the fiction writer must not state things, in quite a lot of instances we hear authorial intrusions that force meaning onto images, as if the images themselves had not been felt as sufficiently easy to understand on their own terms. The end of "A Circle" is one such example, when the narrator links the three boys to the Old Testament prophets.

"A Temple" is clearly in the beginning and in many parts spoken by the inner voice of the child, but various informative elements are provided by an outside omniscient narrator. This is quite clear in the opening page: it is the inner monologue of the child until she is described herself obviously from the outside by a cartoonist: "…she nearly choked on the food she had in her mouth. She doubled over laughing and hit the table with her fist and looked at the two bewildered girls while water started in her eyes and rolled down her fat cheeks and the braces she had in her mouth glared like tin." (237)

That same narrator in the end of the story describes the child and what she sees, which may not be how the child would phrase it herself at this age: the sun as elevated Host drenched in blood. (248)

Nevertheless as the child possesses the same sharp sense of observation for the ridiculous as the narrator who describes her, it is hard to dissociate them. Thus just after the grotesque description of the fat face, we read about Miss Kirby that she "carried her fork delicately in her mouth with one pea on it", from which we immediately infer the kind of stuck up spinster she must be, just before the equally cruel portrait of Mr. Cheatman. A delightful cartoon in a few pen strokes.

Here as in most passages of Flannery O'Connor's fiction the line between inner and outer focalization is too thin for us to be categorical about how focalization works in her stories. One thing is certain however, and it is that Flannery O'Connor was not trying to experiment with narrative techniques. One action or one character will not be perceived through a play on multiple points of view as was already common in her time (as in Faulkner for example).

The narration remains focused on one line of action, or one character seen either through his/her thoughts or seen by one descriptive and at times analytic narrator who may blend with the author. Dialogues are sparsely used, deliberately, so that they are all forceful.

Observation of local manners

Flannery O'Connor stressed the fact that the writer must have a direct link with his/her environment and had to observe and report most exactly what he/she saw. In "The Fiction writer and his country" she wrote that: "fiction begins where human knowledge begins with the senses and every fiction writer is bound by this." Her characters will thus be portrayed first through the sense of perception: they are described in crude terms: "head like a potato…"

Flannery O'Connor also wrote that: "The country the writer is concerned with […] is first objectively the region that surrounds him." Through her everyday environment and its pool of ordinary and mediocre people, she was searching for absolutes, for transcendence. For example, when she chooses a bible salesman or a preacher as protagonist, she is picking up typical Southern characters.

The protagonists are rooted in matter, and this matter is never dissociated from spirit. The stories are immersed in the physical world to move afterwards into the metaphysical plane that is in turn also expressed through the physical realm of death, suffering, fire…

The characters

The names of the characters are similarly charged and fairly often easy to understand: Hazel Motes (a reference to haze, to a foggy brain, and to the "mote one sees in one's neighbor's eyes but not the beam in one's own"), Tarwater (black and in need of purification), but also the Misfit (unadjusted, a social freak), Shiftlet, Shortley, Mr. Head, Mrs. Cope, Mrs. Hopewell… More often than not these characters display some physical deformities that reveal their inner characteristics, and we will analyze them under the heading "the grotesque".

Flannery O'Connor has her characters speak directly to one another or to themselves. As they are for most of them, "simple country people" their conversation is ordinary and they use ready made sentences and popular sayings such as "a good man is hard to find", "good country people", "the life you save may be your own", "the good old days", "in my time [...] children were more respectful of their native states and their parents and everything else. People did right then", the grandmother complains in "A Good Man" (119). "Nothing is like it used to be" (Shiftlet in "The Life", 146). Shiftlet notes that the car he repairs was made in the days when one still knew how to make cars. Now people work on the assembly line and do not care about what they make. It is expensive and does not last.

Many protagonists are children who must bear living with their parents, most often their widowed mother, or their grandfather ("The Artificial Nigger"), or great uncle (*The Violent Bear it Away*). The couple mother-daughter of the stories seems modeled after the one Flannery formed with her authoritarian mother whom one could imagine she crucifies textually by proxy. Apart from the rather shy mother of "A Good Man Is Hard to Find" and the refined and sensitive mother of "A Temple of the Holy Ghost", those adults are hard and mean with the children. Revelation will come for those elder characters as well as for the children.

The relations between the generations are never really "normal"; they are on the contrary very bitter. This seems to be due to their immense pride and their selfishness.

Children do not correspond to the stereotypes of innocent creatures usually encountered in literature. Except for Lucynell and Bevel, all the children harbor some devilish impulses, even the child in "A Temple of the Holy Ghost", supposed to be a persona of the author, who is able to look back on her childhood without pink glasses. Apart from possible personal dislikes, there might be another reason for the impossibility of Flannery O'Connor's children or teenagers to be "nice". The writer was, as we have already seen, a firm believer in original sin. Such a conviction runs counter to the sentimental vision of children as being pure angels, since we are all tainted as soon as we are born, the sin of our ancestors having been passed on to us, until we are finally baptized. Evil is inherent to our human nature, and first appears with original sin, before we even sin willfully. Younger people must, just like adults, come to terms with their being children of God, for even if it is a "given" status, it requires enlightenment to be fully operative.

Fables, allegories, parables

[The following definitions are found in Hegel, *Esthétique, l'art symbolique*. Paris: Aubier, 1964, and in the *Oxford Dictionary of Literary Terms*.]

Flannery O'Connor's stories are not psychologically realistic stories. They veer rather on the fable and the allegory, even though their author said that she never thought "in terms of fable or myth" (*in* Friedman 13), and they are for the most part highly satirical. In the Christian context in which Flannery O'Connor writes, they can be equated with parables or morality plays.

The word **fable** comes from the Latin *fabula*, meaning a story, a tale. Fables are strongly didactic as they are meant to teach under a pleasant garb, easily understandable. It is a story that presents real or well-known facts and gives them a more general meaning, usually through the recourse to animals that behave like humans. Since the characteristics of animals are quite well-known, such as the majesty of the lion, the cunning of the fox, the hard work of ants, the fabulist can avoid using abstractions (cunning, majesty, hard labor), and present these under a concrete form. In the traditional fables, animals however remain a mask and can hinder the right interpretation of the message (Hegel).

More generally now, a fable is "a brief tale in verse or in prose that conveys a moral lesson, usually by giving human speech and manners to animals and inanimate things." *(Oxford Dictionary)* The fable often implies a reversal of situation and Flannery O'Connor's stories display such a structure.

"Fables often conclude with a moral, delivered in the form of an epigram." *(Oxford Dictionary)* An **epigram** is a "wittily condensed expression" in prose or verse. Even though Flannery O'Connor does not write the type of obvious moral lesson one finds, say in La Fontaine, the very last lines of each story do perform the function of an epigram because they always expand the story into a larger vision that definitely contains, even if in a veiled mode, the actual message she aimed at through the plot. O'Connor's works can also be seen as allegories, allegories of the intrusion of the sacred into our every day modern world, for as she puts it: "You should write… about the conflict between an attraction for the holy and the disbelief with anything that has to do with the sacred."

The term **allegory** comes from the Greek, *allêgoria* or "other" and "speak", thus "speaking in using terms other than the proper terms". It is a "story or a visual image with a second distinct meaning partially hidden behind its literal or visible meaning. The principal technique of allegory is personification, whereby abstract qualities are given human shape – as in public statues of Liberty and Justice. An allegory may be conceived as a metaphor that is extended into a structured system. In written narrative, allegory involves a continuous parallel between two (or more) levels of meaning in a story, so that its persons and events correspond to their equivalents in a system of ideas or a chain of events external to the tale: each character and episode in John Bunyan's *The Pilgrim's Progress* (1678), for example, embodies an idea within a pre-existing Puritan doctrine of salvation." (*Oxford Dictionary)*

Because of their names with obvious symbolical meanings, and because of their manners, most of the time stereotypical and easy to identify (pride, blindness, greed, jealousy…), Flannery O'Connor's characters can be seen as allegories of the sins listed in Christian books. In fact, perhaps even more to the point, we can call her stories parables, similar in intent to those Jesus used to teach the crowds around him.

The word comes from the Greek *parabole*, itself from *paraballein*, meaning to throw beside (*para*), to compare (*ballein*). Like the fable, but not through the recourse to animals, the **parable** borrows from the events of every day life, in order to give those events a higher meaning. It is an allegorical tale that originated in the folk tradition of the Orient, to teach through comparisons. The parable goes from the simplest example understandable by every one to a profound significance that can thus be inferred. (Hegel) It leads the mind from the literal level to the highest spiritual one, and is hence a popular form of anagogical didactics.

One can also interpret O'Connor's works as modern **morality plays** for their ingredients perfectly correspond to the definition. These were religious dramas in the 15th and 16th centuries, or "dramatized allegories in which personified virtues, vices, diseases, and temptations struggle for the soul of Man as he travels from birth to death. They instill a simple message of Christian salvation, but often include comic scenes." (*Oxford Dictionary*)

Different layers of interpretation

Anagogy

One must keep in mind that Flannery O'Connor's stories, like most fiction, contain several levels of meaning. In "The Nature and Aim of Fiction", she wrote this about her aesthetics:

> The kind of vision the fiction writer needs to have, or to develop, in order to increase the meaning of his story is called anagogical vision, and that is the kind of vision that is able to see different levels of reality in one image or one situation. The medieval commentators on Scripture found three kinds of meaning in the literal level of the sacred text: one they called allegorical, in which one fact pointed to another; one they called tropological, or moral, which had to do with what should be done; and one they called anagogical, which had to do with the Divine Life and our participation in it. Although this was a method applied to biblical exegesis, it was also an attitude toward all of creation, and a way of reading nature which included most possibilities, and I think it is this enlarged view of the human scene that the fiction writer has to cultivate if he is ever going to write stories that have any chance of becoming a permanent part of our literature. (*Mystery and Manners*, 72-73)

(One also says that the Medieval commentators found four levels, the first one being the literal). An anagogy or anagogue is "a specialized form of allegorical interpretation which reads texts in terms of eschatology." Eschatology is the "theological study or artistic representation of the end of the world. Eschatological writing is found chiefly in religious allegories, but also in some science fiction." *(Oxford Dictionary)*. In French: « anagogie (du grec "qui élève, qui conduit"): terme de théologie. Ravissement de l'âme dans la contemplation des choses divines, ou efforts qu'elle fait pour découvrir le sens mystique de quelques passages de l'Écriture. » Une interprétation anagogique est celle qui « s'élève du sens littéral à un sens spirituel. » (Littré)

Flannery O'Connor's declaration about her intention as to the different layers of meaning she implied in her fiction prompts us to look beyond the mere humorous satire of country people ensconsed in their prejudices. She wants us to move deeper, or higher if you will, towards the mystery of the Incarnation of Christ in the Creation, under aspects which nobody, not even the reader, would expect, probably because we have too narrow an understanding of God's Wisdom.

If, according to her, the writer needs to rely on physical senses, it is to evoke the profound mystery of things, and to help the reader see beyond. What the writer "sees on the surface will be of interest only if he can see through it", or again: "The concrete is necessary but mystery is essential." The reader must pick up the signs in the text that hint at the mystery. These signs are sometimes easy to decipher, sometimes not.

"If the Catholic writer hopes to reveal mysteries, he will have to do it by describing truthfully what he sees from where he is. A purely affirmative vision cannot be demanded of him without limiting his freedom to observe what man has done with the things of God." ("The Church and the Fiction Writer", *America*, March 30, 1957, *in* Friedman v)

The reader must then constantly shift from the literal meaning of what he reads — for example in "The Artificial Nigger" a grandfather taking his grandson to town to show him he knows it well and is thus superior to him — to the symbolical level: they get lost because their hubris blinds them, and they go home humble and thankful to one another for what they have discovered. And then higher still, to the anagogical level: the two men are but God's creatures, proud and silly, thinking they can possess knowledge, but they can only grab a tiny part of Knowledge (as is evidenced in the various revelations they benefit from in the course of their trip), and only once they abandon themselves in the protection of God will they be saved. Through their plight, it is our own fate that is here depicted. We shall explore how anagogy works in "A Temple of the Holy Ghost" in chapter 6.

Satire

Satire is a "mode of writing that exposes the failings of individuals, institutions, or societies to ridicule and scorn." Indirect satire is found in works that allow the readers "to draw our own conclusions from the actions of the characters." (*Oxford Dictionary of Literary Terms*) Satire demands complicity with the reader: it needs a context that the reader recognizes as grotesque, ridiculous, and also an implicit moral standard. Flannery O'Connor's satire operates at the religious and the domestic levels. She makes fun of the vulgarity of American life, for instance when she describes the way people dress, or the cars, the army, the university (the diploma in "A Late Encounter With the Enemy" and the girl with a PhD in "Good Country People"), private property, the family… What she satirizes in religious people is their hypocritical religiosity, their smugness. It can also be the self-complacency of mothers, the indifference of parents ("The River").

Flannery O'Connor's way of expressing satire passes through her narrative mode: in an ironic stance she often paints characters as they picture themselves, usually in an advantageous light, so that we are made to see all their flaws thanks to the distance between what they appear to be and what they think they are. In the opening page of "The Artificial Nigger", she writes "Sixty years had not dulled his responses; his physical reactions like his moral ones, were guided by his will and strong character, and these could be seen plainly in his features." (249) The irony of these lines becomes apparent as soon as he proves unable to find his way in the city. Since her narrative strategy follows the same pattern in all the stories, the reader is quickly made aware of the true nature of the protagonists.

Flannery O'Connor describes ugly details at great length. She shows the contradictions in what people preach and do. And finally she literally slaps them into facing the truth through the violent reversals of situation she provokes. Interestingly, she used to draw cartoons before she turned to writing, and this can really be felt in her narrative mode. She pounds on one or two characteristics of her preys and exaggerates them to lift them above anonymity and normality, and then she hits those people with their now enlarged limbs or props (fiery eyes, hats, wooden legs…) to force them to come to terms with a deeper reality.

Hermeneutic code

The term comes from Hermes (Mercury for the Romans), the god of science, eloquence and cunning, who also acted as the messenger for the other gods. Hermes Trismegistus, or Hermes the thrice greatest, is the name the Greeks gave to the Egyptian god Thot, the founder of alchemy and the occult sciences. The term hermeneutic thus contains all these origins, the idea of something secret, occult, that must be explained and interpreted. Hermeneutics is the science of interpretation, the exegesis, in particular of theological texts, of the biblical

Scriptures, but also of any work of art or text with various layers of meaning that may appear as obscure if one does not possess specific keys.

Flannery O'Connor's stories will only be read on the surface level if the reader does not share the theological foundation in which she grounds her fiction. Aware as she was of the erosion of Christianity in the West and thus of such knowledge by the average reader, in her pact or covenant with her readers, she has introduced in her texts many markers that are fairly easy to detect, clues that will gradually reveal the profound meaning she had in mind. These markers are recurrent from one story to another and allow us to break her hermeneutic code in a rather easy way. Yet, one must be able to see their possible symbolical transformations within the body of her works.

Since the line of reference is Christianity one needs first and foremost to understand the concepts expounded in the beginning of this course. From them stems the meaning of the numerous allusions to vision (eyesight, inner light, dreams), darkness and light, sin and forgiveness, redemption, etc. One then will pay great attention to the symbols and metaphors she uses, many being easy to decode insofar as their meaning is generally shared by western artists: such as eyes (open? closed? sideways?) or glasses.

Natural phenomena, landscape markers are never gratuitously chosen: sun, sunrise, sunset, fire, moon, clouds, rain, trees, rivers, roads, fences, all have symbolical meanings deriving from their link to again Christianity and the action of God in the Creation, or the world. The sun as glory, rain as fertility coming from God, but also as cleansing. The storm unleashed by the turnip-like cloud at the end of "The life You Save May Be Your Own" parodies the all engulfing tornado Shiftlet calls upon God to send on the sinners: he is the one who gets engulfed in it. The river in the story with the same title is, of course, the agent of drowning, but this is only the surface meaning. We have to dive into deeper waters to understand its real significance: it is the river of life in Christ, the river of His Blood, but also of His Baptism, exactly what Bevel sought to undergo. His death is consequently simply apparent since he is now heading towards God.

Similarly the locations where characters chance by, cities, pigsties, snack-bars, filling stations, junk yards… always play a specific function not to be missed, and to which we shall return.

"Treelines" is one of those terms the writer cherishes. As a line, trees raise a barrier, protecting or hiding something and in the text they symbolize the passage between the ordinary and the sacred, or the initiation of characters into something superior, into transcendence.

She also cherishes some universal symbols to which she lends a more personal meaning, for example **peacocks**. They appear so often in her fiction that they have become her trademark. Because of their out-of-this-world beauty, of the specific patterns on their feathers (black eyes or suns surrounded with multicolored ripples), of the circle they form when they spread their tails, these regal birds have been praised in many cultures as solar symbols. In Christendom, they have been seen as representing immortality, Christ's divinity and resurrection. Flannery O'Connor loved them and had many on her farm, wishing to have even more, and they always crop up in her stories to signify the glory of God and to allude to another level of reality.

In "The Life You Save May Be Your Own", Lucynell has "eyes as blue as a peacock's neck" (146): the reader should immediately infer that she is one of those innocent creatures who are already saved since she shares in the divine beauty of these birds. We are also told that her eyes remain "blue even in the dark", which means that she is able to radiate light constantly, like Christ who is Light and has vanquished the world of evil, represented as darkness.

Moreover, the only word Lucynell manages to pronounce (thanks to the providential — in the true sense of the term — arrival of Shiftlet) is "bird", a polysemous word here again, but the most probable meaning must be the reference to the spirit of God, to the freedom of the mind.

In "Good Country People", Hulga is said to be "as sensitive about the artificial leg as a peacock about his tail" (288). However, when the peacock's tail embodies Resurrection, the leg only embodies human hubris. The function of the bible seller will be to make her change her allegiances, from the vanity of a PhD strengthened by the uniqueness of the wooden leg, to the humility of a child of God, accepting as only object of worship the mystery of the Father.

In "The Displaced Person", a peacock appears to signify the glory of God: "'A tail full of suns'… The peacock stood still as if he had just come down from some sun-drenched height to be a vision for them all." (198) Clearly here only the priest who has the right "vision" is able to appreciate immediately the miracle incarnated in the bird, and he twice carefully separates the two parts of the word "beauty-ful" in admiration and awe: "Arrrrrrr!" (198)

The other characters are blind, spiritually, to the bird's manifestation (a word to be taken literally: God made manifest in His Creation): to Mrs McIntyre, the peacock is "Another mouth to feed" (198), and is furthermore, as legend has it, stupidly full of itself, for it raises its tail "Just when it suits him" (198). Mrs. Shortley is just as narrow-minded: "Nothing but a peachicken" (198). The same void in her brain and soul is underlined later, when she pretends to be thinking and is negatively contrasted with the all-seeing eye of God, designed on the feathers of the peacock: "Then she stood a while longer reflecting, her unseeing eyes directly in front of the peacock's tail" (200).

A magnificent description of the tail of the bird follows, but the woman remains insensitive to it because she pretends to be taken up by an "inner vision". The expression usually designates the experience undergone by mystics, or true believers, but here it is devoid of transcendence and full of irony: this vision is smug and less than Christian since it is the vision of the grossly exaggerated — "ten million billion of them" (200) — masses of menacing invaders, the displaced persons fleeing communism in Eastern Europe, heralding the invasion of billions of yellow perils, against which she has to protect her land.

The peacock in this story functions as the signal God places on the path of people to orient them in the proper direction in this time of chaos at the height of the Cold War. Mr. Guizac is Christ sent to the farm to lead the women to perform Charity, one of the theologal virtues at the center of the Catholic life.

Structure

The pattern is not constantly the same but there are many recurrent characteristics. The plot always implies a complete reversal of values, as well as the fulfillment of something brewing from the start.

Each story has a nucleus that is a well-known phrase belonging to the collective unconscious: "A Good Man…", "Good country people"… But these trivial phrases are used as masks, they are deceptive, and either point to the contrary or must be taken far more literally than their users would: a good man in the actual sense of good as opposed to evil in the Christian agenda, is indeed extremely hard to find because we are all eaten up by sin. "The life you save may be your own" means drive carefully, but in speeding away from the women, is Shiftlet actually saving his own life?

The structure often proceeds along these lines:

– The backdrop is described along with the protagonists with their assorted ailments and stupid idiosyncrasies.

– Many have a sense of mission. Or it may be that someone or something (an "opponent") intrudes upon their life. They feel shocked. The protagonists are often fooled by these intruders or by their own reactions to these intruders. They fail to perceive what is going on because they are blinded by their own narrow-mindedness. These episodes are usually very funny ("The River" is one exception).

– The protagonist often perpetrates the denial of salvation or of a Christ-like figure: the Grandmother in "A Good Man Is Hard to Find" denies the fact that Jesus resurrected the dead. Mr. Head (in "the Artificial Nigger") denies knowing his grandson.

– Then, in most cases a drama occurs, always violent, often under the form of sudden death or fire ("The Artificial Nigger" and "A Temple" are rare exceptions). At the last moment, or when they witness someone's death, the protagonists suddenly grasp something, something which will remain vague for the readers if they do not possess the code.

– If they survive physically, the protagonists return to their home base, metamorphosed. Most of the time those who are to receive the light have been searching for it without being actually conscious of their own demands ("A Good Man Is Hard to Find", "The River", "Good Country", "A Temple", "The Displaced Person", *Wise Blood*, *The Violent Bear it Away*...).

In several stories the protagonists suffer from the "troubling and unloved responsibilities of prophecy" and the narrative follows the journey they undertake to try and fulfill this mission. They often return where they left. This long "journey into night" (to paraphrase playwright Eugene O'Neill's title *Long Day's Journey Into Night*) is typically that of the two novels' protagonists: Hazel Motes in *Wise Blood* and Tarwater in *The Violent Bear it Away*, but "The Artificial Nigger" can also be seen as one illustration of this sense of mission.

Whatever their actual plotline, the stories are structured on the pattern of a quest and the characters undergo some form of journey or a displacement of some kind. This pattern is that of most tales narrating the apprenticeship of heroes and heroines (see Propp's *Morphologie du conte*). In order to be fully accepted in the world of adulthood young heroes must leave home, triumph over trials, answer riddles etc., in order to win their loved ones and "live happy ever after." In their quest, they are helped by what we call in French an "adjuvant", or helper, and slowed down or attacked by an "opponent". If the quest is too easy there will not be any real triumph.

In Flannery O'Connor's works, if the structure is similar, the outcome differs in that it is not a question of marrying Prince Charming but encountering the Dragon (as we shall see in the next section) and accepting the judgment of God. In the end an epigram, often enigmatic, rounds up the story and expands it by placing it in the context of world history or the mystery of life: in "A Good Man is Hard to Find", "It's no real pleasure in life" (133); in "The River", "Finally, far downstream, the old man rose like some ancient water monster, and stood empty-handed, staring with his dull eyes as far down the river line as he could see." (174)

Since all characters go on a quest, the reader must carefully interpret the symbolical meaning of the locations they reach. These function as the stages representing each a specific travail, a specific test pilgrims have to triumph over as can be found in allegorical works such as *The Pilgrim's Progress*.

In "The River" one such place requires some explanation: the pigsty. Mrs. Connin's three boys take Bevel around the house to the hog pen full of shoats. The episode builds meaning through the Christian metaphors of the pigs and of revelation. The boys want the innocent child to get a good trampling by the shoats to serve him right. Yet, as usual in the stories, such a mean act will open onto knowledge. So far, Bevel had only seen pink pigs in picture books, stupidly anthropomorphized, with a bow tie. The boys are devilish creatures and play the part of the snake in the Garden of Eden. They tempt him and dare him into doing something that should lead to a discovery: "Now you can lift up the board and...". Suddenly Bevel gets confronted with reality, violently, when the shoat's face pushes into his and then knocks him down and rolls him over in order to kill him. He gains experience and is a child no longer.

Another meaning then surges up: in the Gospel (Luke 8: 26-39; Matthew 8: 28-34; Mark 5: 1-20), Jesus, in the country of Gadarenes, exorcizes a man who is possessed by calling out the legion of demons out of him and throwing them into nearby pigs that go and drown in a lake. Here the demons in the pigs obey the devilish boys and try to defeat the innocent child. However, since he is pure, the demons back down: "The hog ran under the house and subsided, panting..." (162).

"The Artificial Nigger", Flannery O'Connor's favorite story, stages one of the most elaborate quests, structured like Dante's *Divine Comedy*. The hermeneutic code is given in the opening pages when the grandfather proudly imagines himself to be a great guide of men: "He might have been Virgil summoned in the middle of the night to go to Dante, or better Raphael, awakened by a blast of God's light to fly to the side of Tobias." (250) As for the grandchild he is named Nelson, a direct reference to the Admiral under whose valiant command the British fleet won many battles notably the most famous one, Trafalgar, where he met his death, all brilliant human lives having an end.

Though the original purpose of Mr. Head's trip to town, or "his quest", is reversed, since it displays the shame of the two characters, a specific positive quest has nonetheless been accomplished, that of accepting one's humble humanity, and the love of one's kin in the joy of returning home, that is to Paradise.

Like in the *Commedia*, the would-be Virgils go in circles and discover, to their dismay, the different layers of reality in hell and purgatory, as for example when Mr. Head explains the sewer system to the child: "He connected the sewer passages with the entrance to hell and understood for the first time how the world was put together in the lower parts." (204) The dome of the station evokes that of a church, and is their only point of reference. The pair goes from horrifying discoveries (the first negroes...) to dispiriting ones (they are lost...). The irony of this less than divine comedy is that normally in a quest, there are seekers and guides, a Virgil to guide a Dante through the maze of God's intricate world, whereas here the two protagonists pretend to guide the other one, while both are in fact plain seekers of the light. At the end their roles are reversed, the old man resembling "an ancient child" and the child becoming a "miniature old man" (269).

In the book of Tobias, the father and the child are both called Tobias, and their story needs to be summarized here if one wants to understand the reference O'Connor placed in the introductory paragraphs. This Old Testament book does not appear in the Hebraic bible and consequently not in the Protestant one either, but has always been a well-known story (in *Paradise Lost*, Milton features Raphael and the other archangels). It appears in the Apocrypha texts, held by the Catholic Church to be deutero-canonical, or acceptable as canonical.

The elder Tobias was a good man, who was known to bury people according to the proper rites of his people. After various deportations, he again went to bury a dead Jew but the following night bird's droppings fell on his eyes and made him blind. He implored God to grant him death. Elsewhere a woman prayed God also: she had been married seven times and each time a demon, Asmodeus, had killed her new husband.

God summons Archangel Raphael to go and help the two believers. Raphael appears under human form and guides the son of Tobias who is supposed to find the remedy for his father's disease. Raphael advises young Tobias as to the fish he can take and use for this purpose. They finally reach the house of Tobias' cousin, whose daughter is the famous widow. Protected by Raphael, whose advice he closely follows, young Tobias marries her, chases the demon, remains alive, brings the cure back to his father and the whole family rejoices.

The connection to Flannery O'Connor's stories is both in the guide-seeker pair and in the justification for old Tobias's undeserved tragedy. Why should a good servant of god be thus punished? The explanation is given in this line: "It is because you were agreeable to God, that temptation had to try you." (Book of Tobias, 12) Such an explanation echoes the unavoidable passage by the dragon to which we must now turn.

What the stories are structured around: the encounter with the Dragon and Christ

In all the stories, the protagonists undergo a major crisis that involves a confrontation with some strange creature, a man or a statue, or a freak, or a vision. The creatures are hard to interpret, for they can either be avatars of the devil or of Christ.

The earlier editions of *A Good Man Is Hard to Find* were placed under a very interesting epigraph and one wonders why it was removed in the editions published after the author's death. Flannery

O'Connor particularly appreciated these lines by St Cyril of Jerusalem (who lived from around 315 to around 387) and decided that they captured the essence of what she wanted her readers to perceive in her collection of stories, and this is why she had the book open on them:

> The dragon is by the side of the road, watching those who pass. Beware lest he devour you. We go to the father of souls, but it is necessary to pass by the dragon.

Though they sound enigmatic, they become clearer in the Christian context of the belief in evil. Evil is loose in the world, and no one can ignore it, even the saints. The dragon is the physical embodiment of evil, and it pounces on all passers-by. Dragons are fabulous animals, with a giant snake or lizard shape, and seem to have originated in Babylonian mythology, in the story of *Enuma Elish* staging the battle between the Creator and the sea monster. The dragon appears several times in the Old Testament, and in The Book of Revelation (Livre de l'Apocalypse) it specifically designates Satan, the enemy of the Messiah and of the saints. Chapter 5 is devoted to evil and the devil, so here we are just addressing the structural function of the "passing by the dragon".

The second implication of St Cyril's epigraph is that one cannot reach salvation and eternal happiness without some merit. Catholicism and various forms of Protestantism teach that man is free to choose between good and evil, but one way is harder than the other, in this present world. We cannot reach the father of souls, God, without having our mettle tested first through an encounter with the dragon, the archetypal seducer as we shall see later. Thus the pilgrim who forfeits an easy life and earthly pleasures for a difficult exploration of God's design will be rewarded. Eternal bliss can only come at a cost.

All the characters in Flannery O'Connor's stories are sinners, they have all been seduced by the dragon, with a few exceptions, notably that of Bevel in the River. Since in Christianity all men are viewed as sinners, the author writes with her sinful readers in mind: through her entertaining stories, she entices them to identify with her protagonists so that in the end, the readers cathartically experiment grace at the same time it penetrates the characters in a momentous episode.

As we said in the introduction of this section, it is not easy to determine the exact nature of those dragon-like creatures except that they all perform a powerful catalytic role. Many of those figures can be interpreted as being embodiments of Christ, the ultimate helper God sent to His sinful creatures.

We find several examples of a Christ-like figure appearing in an epiphany (revelation of the holy), or a parousia (*parousie* in French, from a Greek term meaning "presence", and designating the return of Christ on earth at the end of time). One of the best examples is of course "A Good Man Is Hard to Find", even though the Misfit refuses the assimilation the grand mother wants to make between himself and the Son of God.

Before encountering the Misfit, the route the family took, under the erring guidance of the grandmother, very distinctly led them to the dragon's hole: Red Sammy's snack bar. The scene is rather easily encoded.

It is a make-believe castle, called The Tower, with a long dark room, the perfect abode for a modern dragon. It specializes in "barbecued sandwiches", denoting intense fire, just like the owner's wife, a "burnt-brown woman". Furthermore the man is called "Red Sammy", again a clear hint at his fiery activities. This "passing by the dragon" is highly proleptic and should have warned the grandmother that the path she had chosen was dangerous: Red Sammy's wife supposes the Misfit may be around and may attack their place; the grandmother uses the token phrase "a good man is hard to find", but it is only perfunctorily here, and the reader senses what is going to happen, though not all the lurid details.

We will have noted that The Tower was a "filling station", that is to say one of those highway altars our materialistic society has erected for our constant and intense devotions to our god, the automobile. Yes, the characters are on a quest, but it can only be "fully-filled" once the fake gods that drink from man-made filling station are destroyed.

In "The River", Harry/Bevel looks at the picture of "a man wearing a white sheet. He had long hair and a gold circle around his head and he was sawing on a board." (161) Afterwards he recalls that he "had been made by a carpenter named Jesus Christ." (163) After such an encounter, it is no wonder he wants to travel down "the River of Life, made out of Jesus' Blood" (165). One may find the story extremely negative since the little boy drowns himself, perhaps for the spite he feels against his careless parents. Nonetheless, if we follow Flannery O'Connor's code, he is undergoing here a baptism, more powerful than any ordinary ones because it is endowed with mystery and plays on the opposition death/life: through his dying the boy cleanses himself, for though he is but a child and has not willfully sinned yet, he is tainted by original sin.

The author chose such a violent act to shock her readers into understanding the importance of the sacrament. She indeed said: "When I write a novel in which the central action is a baptism, I know that for the larger percentage of my readers, baptism is a meaningless rite: therefore I have to imbue this action with an awe and terror which will suggest its awful mystery." ("The role...", in Friedman 33). This remark is justified by the fact that not all her readers came from the South, a region where baptisms are still performed regularly and with great emotional intensity, notably by the Baptists (as seen in the story itself).

In "The Displaced Person", Mr. Guizac is perhaps one of the clearest occurrences of a Christ-like figure intruding upon a self-righteous idiot and transforming her life radically. He has been expelled from his land by war and totalitarianism and is humbly asking for a job to feed his kin. He is the metaphor of the "Other", "one's neighbor" (*son prochain*), or the little children Christ said we should take care of: "What you do unto them, you do it unto me." If one acts badly towards those envoys, one is hard towards God, and if one is good towards them, one is good to God. The accident in which Mr. Guizac is killed reenacts the crucifixion: visually we witness the descent from the cross, a pieta or the entombment: for we see the bent bodies of the whole family of Mr. Guizac leaning over his own dead body.

Yet his death is not important in the economy of the story and, as always in Flannery O'Connor's texts, the meaning of it all must not be misplaced. The tragedy of Mr. Guizac, like that of the Grandmother's family in "A Good Man Is Hard to Find", is not important *per se*, he is already "saved"; his fate, in fact, is not the focus of the story. If the reader lingers on them, it is out of useless sentimentality.

His death triggers the moment of truth for Mrs. McIntyre, who is the real protagonist of the parable. She is the one who must lose what she holds on to in order to be redeemed. The main dramatic element thus in the final passage of the story is the complete transformation the death of the Polish man/Christ provokes for his employer.

She swooned when she saw the accident and then lost her memory not only of the recent past but also of everything. She who was a very organized "master woman" is now totally unable to act rationally: the hectic pace of the first sentences reproduces her running around without any efficiency. The author empties her, so to speak, so that she can be filled anew with God's grace: she is punished for her sins (love of material possessions, moral superiority, racism, etc.) and loses everything, much like the grandmother in "A Good Man Is Hard to Find".

Yet, her shock at seeing the man killed makes her receptive, for salvation and grace will be forced down her brain and soul.

Mrs. McIntyre, through the mystery of transformation, becomes a "Displaced Person", she feels she is in a foreign country… She must experience the same suffering the Guizacs have been undergoing all their lives. She loses not only her farm, but all the people working for her. On the contrary, Mr. Guizac dies with all his family around him, as if they all formed one single body, a metaphor for the whole Church. Though the Guizacs do not own any material wealth, they possess the strength of love. The father will be missed, they will cry for him, whereas nobody will miss Mrs. McIntyre.

Sulk and Mr. Shortley leave her because they feel the doom now attached to the farm and see that she has lost all power over them. Only one person remains at her side, a colored woman, in another reversal of things since she hated black people… She loses all her physical capacities, but in fact the message is that she can thus open her heart. She loses her eyesight but has a new inner sight, her spiritual vacuum is day after day filled by the regular teaching of the priest. The final line is very amusing because it implies a sort of ironical punishment: now Mrs. McIntyre cannot refuse to listen to the priest.

It also shows the patience of the priest (he is the only one who bothers to visit her) who is on a mission: enforcing the unrelenting power of God who grants grace to the most miserable creatures, even those who are rejected by everyone because they themselves were unbearable, and He does so through His Church: note the capital letter of the very final word ("Church") that is not only the last word of the story DP, but of the whole book *A Good Man Is Hard to Find*. Since it is the very last word we read, its influence is paramount and this is the final message Flannery O'Connor wanted her readers to take home when they closed the book.

The life-changing encounters may involve strange creatures that are neither properly speaking the dragon or Christ, but weird phenomena, such as the hermaphrodite or the statue of a nigger.

In "A Temple of the Holy Ghost", the encounter is indirect and occurs thanks to the child's listening to her cousins at night and then recreating a specific vision, that of the hermaphrodite they saw in the tent in the circus. The mystery of such an extraordinary being confronts the child to the mystery of creation, and the repeated words of the monster "God made me thisaway" force her to admit her own condition as a creature of God and thus His Incarnation in herself and the whole creation.

The artificial nigger is the strangest example of such encounters in the stories. The statue Mr. Head and his grandson discover in their endless circles is first of all a preposterous proof of racism. A reification of Blacks, it is one of those life-size statues that used to adorn shops or lounges. More meanings develop: it is crumbling and miserable, its outside appearance echoing the state of mind of the onlookers, and it is the same size as Nelson, thus confronting him with his black double. Furthermore the putty that is supposed to hold it to the wall has cracked, pretty much like the putty supposed to hold Nelson together, his grandfather.

The statue allows a holy vision, as would a statue in a Catholic church (Protestant churches have no statues). It is meant to teach something. Like the pair of seekers, the artificial nigger has an impaired vision/eyesight: one eye is white, and bad. It also implies a profound conundrum: "They stood gazing at the artificial negro as if they were faced with some great mystery, some monument to another's victory that brought them together in their common defeat." (269) The victorious other is God, triumphing over the devil who sowed the seeds of hatred and treason in the two men's souls. By admitting this defeat and their frailty, they are both redeemed and can start anew on their life journey.

3

The mark of the South

The South has been (with New England until the twentieth century) one of the most fertile producers of writers, and Flannery O'Connor belongs to a rich community alongside with Edgar Poe, William Faulkner, Eudora Welty, Carson McCullers, William Styron, Truman Capote, William Goyen, Tennessee Williams... There are reasons to this, and they are the factors that have made the South different from the other sections.

The historical factor

Flannery O'Connor explained that one reason why that region was so prolific was that it was still (until her time at least) stable, closed on itself and somehow reassuring within the constantly shifting American society. She said that the writer who does not feel the need to move out of his/her home area could spend more time on his/her writing.

The other reason is that the South lost the Civil War and never fully recovered from this defeat. However it forced it to grow out of the bland innocence the rest of the country basked in. It experienced evil through slavery, the original sin of the United States. Its Fall taught it the limits of human perfection and instilled an acute feeling of metaphysical anxiety in its writers.

The constant cohabitation of two antagonistic races also whetted the keen sense of observation of these artists who could witness strong and violent social interactions right in front of them.

The religious factor

The South of the USA is the stronghold of the Bible Belt, a nickname given by Mencken to this vast region including not just the South but also parts of the Midwest, because of the constant display of the Bible by thousands of preachers on the streets, in churches, on the radio or now television. The dominant religion of the Bible Belt is Protestantism in its Evangelist, or now Evangelical form. This movement itself includes a great variety of groups united by their intense religious practice and profound respect for the Bible accepted literally: Baptists (themselves divided into several groups, the largest being that of "The Southern Baptists", counting now over sixteen million members), Methodists, Pentecostals… The most conservative among them belong to the Fundamentalist movement (the name Fundamentalism comes from a book, *The Fundamentals: a Testimony to the Truth,* published in 1910 and containing the results of various meetings of Presbyterian and Baptist evangelists who wanted to return to old time values and to what they imagined to be the foundation of Christianity, the primitive Church).

Though the religious and social landscape is now changing, Catholicism has always been a minority denomination in the South, and definitely was so in Flannery O'Connor's lifetime. She devoted an essay to her situation: "A Catholic novelist in the Protestant South." The Catholic Church was identified as the Scarlet Whore described in the Book of Revelation (Livre de l'Apocalypse; chapter 17) and the term "Christian" could not apply to its members.

Her opinion on her fellow Southerners was complex: she wanted to assert what she felt to be the superiority of the Catholic interpretation of the world, and was very militant about it, while at the same time she admired the drive and conviction of the Evangelists, far closer to God than most Americans, or most Westerners for that matter, who already experienced life in a post-Christian world and would not be troubled by spiritual questionings. Therefore, she peopled her stories with the likes of the preachers everywhere to be encountered in the South, whereas there are not many Catholics in her stories.

Flannery O'Connor felt however that Protestant preachers relied on the Scriptures, on the printed Word too much and not enough on the mysteries of Incarnation, of the Creation and of Grace, and that they used the name of Jesus more as a sort of empty mantra than as a profound worship for Him. Yet, they were living in a God-thirsty world, and she would help them go in the right direction.

In 1959 she wrote that in fact Catholics and Fundamentalists were closer together than the latter were to the other Protestants who had become too secularized: "It is an embarrassment to our fundamentalist neighbors to realize that they are doctrinally nearer their traditional enemy, the Church of Rome, than they are to modern Protestantism. The day may come when Catholics will be the ones who maintain the spiritual traditions of the South?" (*in* Wood 13) (Strangely enough, even if this tradition still remains heavily Protestant, recent developments have proved her statement true and on many issues conservative Catholics have now become the bedfellows of the Protestant conservatives).

She herself said:

> The Catholic novelist in the South is forced to follow the spirit into strange places and to recognize it in many forms not totally congenial to him. But the fact that the South is the Bible Belt increases rather than decreases his sympathy for what he sees. His interest will in all likelihood go immediately to those aspects of Southern life where the religious feeling is most intense and where its outward forms are farthest from the Catholic... ("The Role of the Catholic Novelist", *Greyfriar. In* Friedman 32)

In an interview with Granville Hicks she said: "I'm not interested in the sects as sects; I am concerned with the religious individual, the backwoods prophets. Old Tarwater is the hero of *The Violent Bear It Away*, and I am right behind him 100 per cent." (*in* Hyman 39). Or again:

> People make a judgment of fanaticism by what they are themselves. To a lot of Protestants I know, monks and nuns are fanatics, none greater. And to a lot of monks and nuns I know, my Protestants prophets are fanatics. For my part, I think the only difference between them is that if you are a Catholic and have this intensity of belief you join the convent and are heard no more; whereas if you are a Protestant and have it, there is no convent for you to join and you go about the world getting into all sorts of trouble and drawing the wrath of people who don't believe anything much at all down on your head. This is one reason why I can write about Protestant believers better than Catholic believer — because they express their belief in diverse kinds of dramatic action which is obvious enough for me to catch. (*in* Hyman, 40)

Hyman summarizes then her words thus: she chose "Protestant Fundamentalism as her metaphor for Catholic vision... it was a brilliant choice. It gave her imagery that is naturally dramatistic [...] and

[...] it freed her from the constraint of good taste" since she could invent lurid scenes (as in *Wise Blood*) not proper for nuns...

Again in a letter Flannery O'Connor listed the advantages of writing as a Catholic in the South:

> Now the South is a good place for a Catholic literature in my sense for a number of reasons.
> 1. In the South belief can still be made believable and in relation to a large part of the society. We are not the Bible Belt for nothing.
> 2. The bible being generally known and revered in the section, gives the novelist that broad mythical base to refer to that he needs to extend his meaning in depth.
> 3. The South has a sacramental way of life...
> 4. The aspect of Protestantism that is most prominent (at least to the Catholic) in the South is that of man dealing with God directly, not through the mediation of the church, and this is great for the Catholic novelist like myself who wants to get close to his character and watch him wrestle with the Lord. (*in* Hyman 40-41)

Trying to discern what marks Flannery O'Connor's stories as Catholic and not as Protestant is extremely difficult because what the author shows are Protestants and Catholics alike confronted with grace. Now, as we have seen in chapter 2, grace for the Catholics could be obtained through good works (added of course to God's desire to grant it). For Protestants, who rebelled against such a proud assumption from the part of the Catholics (because no one could actually force God to do something, and one could not "buy" grace), grace can only be granted by God as He wishes. In the stories, it seems fairly obvious that not many characters are accomplishing good deeds to win grace. They are instead nasty and mean. Thus the grace they suddenly receive falls into the Protestant "category". Perhaps the distinction between the two doctrinal views is to be found in the link of the characters to their community.

Louis Rubin wrote that:

> The ways of the fundamentalist South, especially in its more primitive levels of religious experience, are not those of the Roman Catholic Church. Primitive Protestantism in the South is puritanical, much more so than the Presbyterian Church itself is nowadays; the struggle against Satan is individual, continuous and desperate, and salvation is a personal problem, which comes not through ritual or sacrament, but in the gripping fervor of immediate confrontation with eternity. The rural South is not so much Christ-centered as Christ-haunted. PREPARE TO MEET THAT GOD, the signs along the highway counsel the motorist, and WHERE WILL YOU SPEND ETERNITY? (*in* Friedman 50, and see Wood's book precisely entitled *Flannery O'Connor and the Christ-Haunted South*).

Flannery O'Connor is fascinated by the solitary struggle between her Protestant protagonists and their God since they do not have mediators in between.

Being mostly Protestant then, her haunted characters search grace individually, but it might be their creator's Catholicism which forces them to receive it through a violent rite or a sacrament (as in "The River") and to return, morally altered for the better, in their community from which they used to stand out: Mrs McIntyre, Hulga probably once she manages to climb back to her mother, the child and her mother in "A Circle in the Fire", Nelson and his grandfather in "The Artificial Nigger". They have "swallowed" their pride and are now humbled by the great mystery revealed to them.

As with all great works, Flannery O'Connor's immersion in one particular region makes it universal. Even when she describes the bizarre creatures of Southern small towns and rural areas, she dwells on the condition of modern man in our Western world. The Fall of the South is that of our society in general. Flannery O'Connor feels that God has entrusted her with the mission to wake up people, to make them understand and accept the redeeming work of grace.

Satirizing Southern myths

Even though she was dedicated to her home area, she constantly debunked its self-deluding myths, such as gallantry, gentility and chivalry. She hated Margaret Mitchell, the epitome of the Southern Belle novelist, and what she wrote (*Gone with the Wind*) and what she stood for. The allusion to "Gone With the Wind" in front of graves by the roadside, as well as the ruined plantation in "A Good Man Is Hard to Find" testify to Flannery O'Connor's scorn for such literature and values.

She cleanses the mind of *ante-bellum* illusions. The landladies of her stories are no Southern Belles even if they feel proud of their properties: the grandmother in "A Good Man Is Hard To Find", the women in "The Displaced Person", "The Life You Save May Be Your Own", "Good Country People" in which Mrs. Hopewell thinks "Mrs. Freeman was a *lady*" (272), while her daughter stands for a parody of the celebrated Southern debutantes.

"A Late Encounter with the Enemy" is probably the best satire of *ante-bellum* Southern society's military establishment, beauty pageants and college institutions. Sally puts on her most beautiful attire "because she was supposed to go up on the stage", as befits the beauty pageant requirements. But the end of the sentence, an anticlimax, reveals that it is simply in order to keep the great war hero from falling for he keeps trying to march. (137) Both heroes are too old for what they are being decorated for: she receives a BA at 64, and he a speech at 104.

"Good Country People" denounces the other great fallacy of the South, its worship of the bible (which is a displacement from the worship of God), through the fabulous suitcase of the bible salesman. His bibles are only boxes containing the temptations of the world: alcohol, gambling cards, lust (here as a medicine or condoms against venereal disease) (289-290).

Racism

The attitude of the Whites towards the Blacks is specifically denounced in "The Artificial Nigger", not so much through the statue itself as in the train episode and in the Black districts of the city. Ironically, Nelson is in the beginning color-blind since he can't even recognize the Blacks on the train. It is only when his grandfather makes fun of him that he starts hating the Black man, although it is more because he was mocked by his grandfather than out of genuine hatred. The social pattern of racism is quite cleverly denounced in this passage.

The reversal of the Southern order of things in the city is also quite interesting, and Flannery O'Connor's satire resembles that of William Faulkner for whom only the Blacks are saved and enduring. In the short story, it is the Blacks who tell the epitome of the proud and all-knowing White which way to go. Furthermore, the child who has never had a mother to take care of him, falls for a large colored woman who in his eyes embodies the Mother, before being confronted with his Black brother in the statue.

The encounter with the rich Black Man, the fat woman and then the statue are just as many stages in the process of gradual revelation as the marks of a radically anti-racist manifesto, for even though Flannery O'Connor was horrified by segregation and racism, her design went beyond the mere righting of such wrongs.

4

The grotesque and revelation

The term "grotesque" comes from the Italian "grottesca", from "grotta". It applied to the scenes painted on walls by the Romans and discovered during the excavation of "grottoes", in particular the Thermal Baths of Titus in Rome.

There are various kinds of grotesques in Western literature. Roughly speaking one category encompasses the bizarre characters embodying disorder, the reversal of values and they are joyous and funny. We find them in carnivals and in Rabelais for example. The Russian critic Bahktin has analyzed them as the life force in our culture. Carnavalization is a positive process which cleanses society of its stagnating hierarchies and values.

The other kind of grotesque is the one found in a great number of American works of fiction. The grotesque shocks us because it is a violation of normal expectations. Another term is freak. These creatures derived from medieval carnivals reappeared in Gothic literature not to amuse the readers but to scare them, under the guise of monsters, perverts, abnormal beings. Frankenstein's monster is such a freak. Their significance is not always easy to fathom. Frankenstein's monster, for one, is horrible but he is in fact extremely moving and heart rending. The freaks of Edgar Poe are not of the same kind: they most often represent decay, their physical decrepitude translating their moral decadence and despair. Dickens loved portraying odd characters as well to show the vices of society.

In our time, freaks are mostly an American literary and filmic production. The list is long from Sherwood Anderson in his famous *Winesburg, Ohio*, Steinbeck's *Of Mice and Men* to *King Kong* (the heir of Poe's *Murder in the Rue Morgue*)… They greatly characterize Southern literature in which they often stand for the fallen state of grace the South has never fully recovered from. Some authors use them to appeal to our sentimentality, like Carson McCullers. Hers, like Anderson's and Steinbeck's, are lonely people who have turned into physical and psychological freaks because they were rejected by society. They are alienated anti-heroes in need of love and the by-products of a careless world. Faulkner has a passion for freaks as well. A great number of his characters belong to the genre but are also quite remote from those of McCullers. They are lost souls, decaying with the society around them, in search of spirituality or plainly the incarnation of evil.

The freaks of Flannery O'Connor's fiction are the exact opposite of those of Carson McCullers whom she did not like for she always hated sentimentality. Flannery O'Connor said that if Southern writers have a penchant for freaks it is because they are able to recognize them! "To be able to recognize a freak you have to have some conception of the whole man, and in the South the general conception of man is still in the main theological." ("Some aspects of the Grotesque in Southern Literature", quoted *in* Friedman, 276)

Perhaps because she was raised in the South, Flannery O'Connor felt very early a personal fascination for the bizarre. She favored peacocks, chickens and swans which were deformed. This attraction started when as a child of five she had had an extraordinary chicken which could walk backward… and a film crew had come to film it. (Delta 4).

This passion remained with her. One of Flannery O'Connor's favorite stories is Hawthorne's "The Birthmark". It is the story of a beautiful woman who has an ugly red stain on her face. Her husband through a little bit of witchery manages to erase it but as soon as the lady's beauty is perfect, and she is no longer grotesque, she dies.

In "The Fiction Writer and His Country" she states: "…writers who see by the light of their Christian faith will have, in these times, the sharpest eye for the grotesque, for the perverse, for the unacceptable." (*in* Friedman 108) Or elsewhere she wrote: "The direction of many of us will be toward concentration and the distortion that is necessary to get our vision across […] The problem of such a novelist will be to know how far he can distort without destroying and in order not to destroy he will have to go far down into himself to reach those underground springs that will give rank to his work." ("Some aspects of the Grotesque in Southern Literature" *in* Friedman 279)

How does she portray her freaks? Friedman wrote: "She has a kind of Dickensian devotion to oddity." (11) With a keen sense of observation for the most slightly deviant details Flannery O'Connor has built an incredibly funny cast of characters. She treats human beings as if they were a farm menagerie and it is always those who present some kind of particularity, of deformity, which she is most interested in. This is what she calls the "distortion of characters". (Delta 4)

They have one leg only, are blind, deaf, mute…

They look like:

– birds: the grandmother in "A Good Man Is Hard to Find" "raised her head like a parched old turkey hen crying for water" (132)

– animals: "A Temple of the Holy Ghost": the boys "sat like monkeys, their knees on a level with their shoulders and their arms hanging down between." (240); one of the boys has a "dog-like loving look" (240); or at the end of the same story: the child "noted that his ears were pointed almost like a pig's." (248); the mother in "A Good Man Is Hard to Find" has a head kerchief tied as "rabbit's ears". (117)

– vegetables: again this mother's face is "broad and innocent as a cabbage" (117)

We can almost visualize her stories as paintings by Jerome Bosch or Pieter Brueghel. They stick to our retina. The cruelty they imply strikes the imagination far more efficiently than the whining freaks of Anderson.

Flannery O'Connor's freaks do not all play the same function. For some, their grotesqueness marks them as the complacent and uncaring members of society. Yet these strange characteristics are pathways to grace because their physical deformities are a concrete representation of the evil present in all of us.

Such a belief is very ancient and in literature physical defects have often mirrored moral defects. Grotesqueness denotes our evil nature. In the Christian economy of grace, it is the presence of evil that justifies the necessity of redemption. "Sin and the grotesque are joined because sin violates the cosmic order." (Friedman 108)

In many other cases the grotesques are the adjuvants, the catalysts which make the protagonist understand things, and sometimes they are even Christ figures themselves, the hermaphrodite of "The Temple" being one of the best examples, whereas the ugly looking child this story opens on is self-righteous and, overlooking her own ugliness, scorns other people's oddities.

Or it can be the grotesqueness of the protagonists themselves, a lurid or disgusting detail, which triggers their own moment of revelation: Hulga and her wooden leg form a grotesque character and it is through the leg that the girl is taught a lesson. In "The Temple of the Holy Ghost", it is the stinking sweat of Alonso that prompts the child's contemplation of God. We may see in this a definitely Catholic vision of mankind. For the Catholics, the whole of Creation is holy, even its lowest forms, whereas in many forms of Protestantism there exists a hierarchy with the Elect standing above the fray. The Elect, or the Chosen People is a view deriving from the Hebrews' vision of themselves as God's People and is not a Catholic perspective. The Southern Baptists and Fundamentalists who found Churches at every street corner share this view that they alone are the Elect in the eyes of a vengeful God. Such an attitude is minutely narrated in Flannery O'Connor's two novels.

Also we must ponder on one of her most quoted statements about the need to distort in order to find the truth: "The prophet is a realist of distances, and it is this kind of realism which goes into great novels. It is a realism which does not hesitate to distort appearances in order to show a hidden truth." ("The Role of the Catholic Novelist". *Greyfriar*, 1964, *in* Friedman 157)

Again in a lecture she gave in 1960 on "Some aspects of the Grotesque in Southern Literature" she said:

> In nineteenth-century American writing, there was a good deal of grotesque literature, which came from the frontier and was supposed to be funny, but our present grotesque characters, comic though they are, are at least not primarily comic. They seem to carry an invisible burden; their fanaticism is a reproach, not merely an eccentricity. I believe that they come about from the prophetic vision peculiar to any novelist, but particularly and in these times deliberately peculiar to the novelist (interested in mystery). In the novelist's case prophecy is a matter of seeing near things with their extensions of meaning; and thus of seeing far things close up. The prophet is a realist of distances, and it is this kind of realism that you find in the best modern instances of the grotesque [...] In any case it is when the freak can be sketched as a figure to our essential displacement that he attains some depth in our literature. (*in* Friedman 275)

Violence

In most cases the encounter with grace is achieved through violence. In *Mystery and Manners* Flannery O'Connor wrote: "In my own stories I've found that violence is strangely capable of returning my characters to reality and preparing them to accept their moment of grace." This violence at times verges on the burlesque and makes the reader smile (death of the grandmother in "A Good Man Is Hard to Find", the stolen wooden leg in "Good Country People"…), but it can also be cruel and dramatic without any kind of humor in it: the child drowning in the river, the tractor running over the displaced person… Yet Flannery O'Connor never indulges in the actual physical suffering provoked by violence. Hers is exclusively a catalyst to reach into the mystery of the divine.

Violence has always been used in literature because it exists in life. What differs from one author to the other is the symbolical use he/she will derive from it. In America there has been a long tradition of "Regeneration through violence", brilliantly analyzed by Richard Slotkin in the book bearing this title. It was above all the violence on the frontier from the early years of the colonies until the nineteenth century. However, it was mostly the kind of violence one inflicted on the enemy, or the one the enemy inflicted on oneself and that one was able to triumph over because of one's moral superiority (with God one one's side), which regenerated the heroes and purified society.

Flannery O'Connor seems to have borrowed the technique but her strategy is different: violence is not to be triumphed over, it must be accepted for it transforms the individual for ever. It is not a question of courage, of enduring duress, but of abandoning everything one held on to before in order to be engulfed in the mystery of redemption. Her violence is akin to that of the apocalypse: final, not compassionate, but forever subsuming all things.

Grotesqueness, meanness, violence and atonement in "A Good Man Is Hard to Find"

The title of this story comes from a musical by Eddie Green, about a woman looking through a window and reading a paper for matrimonial ads, looking for a good man. The meaning can be expanded to mean "a good citizen", or later "a good Christian". The story is divided between the good people, those who belong to the same class as the grandmother, who have good blood and the others. Yet the separation is illusory since, as we know, the grandmother only pretends to be a lady, much like Blanche Dubois in Tennessee Williams' *A Streetcar Named Desire* (1947).

Self-centeredness as the mark of the grotesque

One can argue about who is grotesque in "A Good Man Is hard to Find". If the Misfit seems to correspond to the definition, the grandmother qualifies in reality just as well for that definition. She is ridiculed from the start because she is selfish and stubborn, and we immediately come to wish she were taught a lesson. It is in fact quite hard to accept Flannery O'Connor's violence against the innocent members of her family, unless it is to show us that the grandmother is really mean since she does not even feel sorrow at their deaths, only fear in front of her own fate. The author wants us to focus exclusively on her and discard our superficial fondness for the rest of the family who are just stick figures in her stratagem.

The self-centeredness of the misfit is thus rivaled by that of the old lady: the declarative clauses of the very first line of the story express her adamant will: "The grandmother didn't want to go to Florida. She wanted..." The repetition of "want" once in the negative form, the other in the positive, implies that she will be the focus of the plot because she is the one whose desires have to be obeyed. The next page is again completely focused on her, what "she" wears, what "she" says... She constantly tries to exert power on the other members of her family: "She was seizing at every chance to change Bailey's mind" (3rd line)

The next day she is the first one in the car which implies that she only took care of herself and has not helped in the house (again a rather common phenomenon...).

She carries a valise, a grotesque one that looks like a hippopotamus. We must remember that valises in Flannery O'Connor's fiction are clues to be deciphered. Under an innocent cover they hide evil things. In "A Temple of the Holy Ghost", the suitcases the two young girls carry contain the profane clothes they put on as soon as they quit their more "sacred", or at least more modest, brown convent uniforms: "as soon as they opened their suitcases [...] they [...] put on red skirts and loud blouses." (236) Red is here the color of lust, of sin.

Bailey, the grandmother's son can also be seen as a freak: he is a rather dull character easily manipulated by his mother as is shown in his physical posture indicating he is in between two straight positions, not deciding whether to be sitting up or standing up: "sitting on the edge of his chair", typically reading the sports page while remaining passive.

The grandmother lies as to her motivation for not going to Florida, and the reader instinctively senses that she will be punished for this lie.

Fake Southern gentility

Even though she could be any kind of woman, her attitude towards the Blacks is typical of old Southern mentalities: "Little niggers in the country don't have things like we do" (119), or they are so stupid that one of them ate the watermelon with E.A.T. on it. (120) She is also sorry she did not marry the E.A.T. man for he became a millionaire with his Coca-Cola stocks, Coca-Cola being one of the rare famous Southern companies in those days.

Her gentile ladyhood transpires through her sophisticated clothes, radically different from those of the mother. Even though they are just going to sit in the car for most of the day (the mother and the kids are in slacks) the old lady is dressed to kill (or be killed!): "but the grandmother had on a navy blue straw sailor hat with a bunch of white violets on the brim and a navy blue dress with a small white dot in the print. Her collars and cuffs were white organdy trimmed with lace and at the neckline she had pinned a purple spray of cloth violets containing a sachet. In case of an accident, anyone seeing her dead on the highway would know at once that she was a lady." (118) (a sachet is a little pouch containing perfume)

The narrative voice goes from an outside description of the clothes to, in the last sentence, the inner monologue of the lady. This sentence functions also as a prolepsis, a comical one since none of the expectations of the grandmother will be fulfilled, except the very staging of the accident: it will not be a highway but a dirt road; she will be broken up like a puppet in a pool of blood, not very ladylike.

The colors chosen by the grandmother belong to the register of the uniform of elegant women: white, navy blue and purple. Unlike those of the mother which are casual and seen by the narrator as linking her to nature (*as* a cabbage, *like* a rabbit), the old lady has chosen her attire and the violets on purpose to imitate nature, to ape it in its colors and intricacies. The landscape they drive through displays the same colors: "the trees were full of silver-white sunlight [...] the blue granite [...] rows of green lace-works [...] the brilliant red clay banks streaked with purple". (the paragraph after the description of her clothes, 119) She does not wear any red yet, but in the end the parallel with nature will be complete for she will turn red in the face.

Claude Richard in one of the best analyses of the story, "Désir et destin in 'A Good Man Is Hard to Find'", wrote:

> La grand-mère peut donc apparaître comme un objet culturel singeant la nature, mais privée de la couleur qui porte promesse de récoltes (le vert), c'est-à-dire privée de capacité de devenir. On comprend mieux alors son hostilité envers la Floride, terre des fleurs (naturelles) et de la floraison, c'est-à-dire d'une éclosion que, forte de son bagage culturel passéiste (*'In my time'–Gone With the Wind*), elle récuse. (Delta 65)

The only natural thing she carries is the cat, but as we all know cats are domesticated and removed from the true world of nature. The one here is hidden so that he is part of the grandmother's deceptive stratagem. It is the cat that provokes the accident by reverting to its natural state (after she has upset the valise): he "sprang on Bailey's shoulder [...] clang to his neck like a caterpillar." (124-125)

The function of the car

The fact that the grandmother sits in the back of the car is important. In Flannery O'Connor's fiction cars play a paramount function: though they are man-made machines, and condense our materialistic and consumerist culture, they always prepare their passengers to receive a mystic revelation.

The father and mother sit in the front. The mother is part of the natural world as was made clear by the description in the first page: she looks like a cabbage, green kerchief tied like a rabbit's ears; she is "innocent" as well as the baby and to a certain measure her husband, hence their fate causes no actual problem in the strategy of grace.

On the back seat, one finds the children and the old woman. They all belong to the cultural order, not the natural one. The girl's name, June Star, may evoke the cosmos but it is rather meant to link her to the Hollywood stars. The grandson, somehow freakish ("stocky child with glasses") bears the name of John Wesley, the founder of Methodism, one of the major Protestant religions of the USA. Derision may also be present here, even though the boy is quite clever and perceptive, and there is another evil John Wesley in "A Later Encounter". In any case he belongs to the cultural world like his sister because they read comics, play and fight (131), they are quite keen to visit the plantation: they "began to yell and scream that they wanted to see the house…" (120)

From the back of the car which signifies backwardness and meanness, the accident (that she caused herself) will make the grandmother fly onto the front seat, the place of natural people and of simple understanding. It is almost the final stage in her initiation: "the mother clutching the baby, was thrown out of the door onto the ground" (we have seen she is natural herself and does not have to fear her fate); "the old lady was thrown into the front seat… she was curled up under the dashboard." (125) She wanted to be the actual driver of the car but now is trying to make amends and reverts to the position of a child (curled up), which announces the one she will have in death. Now she cannot hide at the back. It is the final acting out of her life of whims and lies, she is to face her maker. (See Richard, 69)

The dragons

In the chapter on structure we saw how the stories always followed a quest pattern, that is a journey hindered by obstacles. "A Good Man Is Hard to Find" exemplifies this best. The grandmother must meet the dragons announced in the epigraph.

We have seen that Red Sammy was portrayed as a dragon-like man: he is red, (repeated twice), he lives in the middle of the woods in a strange house, looking more like a cavern, his wife is burnt-brown. The grandmother triumphs over his probable meanness (or his desire to slap the insulting little girl) by talking with him in conventional terms using exclusively ready made sentences about the good old days and she flatters him "you're a good man" (122). But it is the last time she can triumph. Her next dragon will not be soothed as easily. Fittingly, the woods open behind the Misfit and his men as if they were a dragon's mouth: "the line of woods gaped like a dark open mouth." (138)

She cannot fool him because he immediately corrects her. She wants to be pitied and pretends they have "turned over twice", but he coldly retorts: "Oncet". Her calling him a good man does not work. It is again her stupidity that provokes their death since if she had not shouted that she recognized him he might not have had to kill them (and it would have been another story!)

She gradually loses all her attributes of gentility: first the cat (thrown by Bailey), her hat, her family, her voice. Unlike in the beginning when she "wanted" or "did not want" things, she now "found that she had lost her voice" (131). She is no longer active but sees herself as if she had already left her body, and is thus ready to receive grace. Just before losing her last weapon, she mumbles Jesus several times. Amusingly she said it as if she were cursing, and this sacrilege, or simply the name of Jesus, prompts the Misfit to deliver his anti-sermon on Jesus, much in the same manner as Hazel Motes (in *Wise Blood*) who founded the Church Without Christ. The Misfit is a fanatic who believes that things would have turned differently had Jesus done what he preached:

> "Jesus was the only One who raised the dead," [...] "and He shouldn't have done it. He thrown everything off balance. If He did what He said, then it's nothing for you to do but throw away everything and follow Him, and if He didn't then it's nothing for you to do but enjoy the few minutes you got left the best way you can – by killing somebody or burning down his house or doing some other meanness to him. No pleasure but meanness." (132)

When the old lady answers: "Maybe He didn't raise the dead", he retorts that he would have liked to have been present then so that he would now know for sure and "I wouldn't be like I am now." (132)

His spending time killing people and burning things (what quite a lot of Flannery O'Connor's characters actually do) is planned to redress the balance of good Jesus said he was bringing on earth. Some critics have seen the Misfit as representing Jesus since it is through him that the lady is granted grace, but his denial of the historical Jesus makes this interpretation hard to sustain. He is more like a dragon working for Jesus, but not replacing him. Or again he can be seen thus: "...the Misfit as antagonist embodies *both* demonic and Christ-like potentialities". (Desmond 31)

His wearing a hat has been interpreted as denoting his deviousness. Funnily enough, when some students asked Flannery O'Connor about its significance, she answered: "The significance of the Misfit's hat is to cover The Misfit's head." (*in* Ralph Wood, ix)

What is stressed also in the story is the necessity to have a proper vision, in an actual and symbolical sense. The Misfit is someone who only believes what he can see: he has seen the accident and knows the car only turned once: "We seen it happen", so that the old lady cannot fool him. He regrets not having been able to see Jesus raise the dead, for then he would not have needed to doubt His divinity. Flannery O'Connor implies here that a good eyesight is not sufficient to reach the proper vision of the divine mystery.

In spite of this chink in his armor, the Misfit fulfils a positive function for he redresses the balance of power and humiliates the once so proud lady. "The Grandmother's rude displacement from her lofty vision of herself as a morally superior 'lady' is brought about by her meeting with the Misfit." (Desmond 30)

The grandmother, who had earlier begged the Misfit to pray Jesus, now disowns Him, much like Saint Peter did in his three denials of Jesus: "Maybe He didn't raise the dead." (132) Incidentally it is then almost at once that the Misfit shoots her precisely three times.

The end is quite delicate to explain. We understand easily the fact that as a talker she deserved a lesson (satisfying every reader), but we don't grasp so clearly her calling the Misfit "you are one of my babies. You're one of my children!" (132). She seems so full of motherly love that it sounds somehow weird, unless the author wanted us to see how grace can transform people: obviously she did not care for her son and family, she can't even remember whose shirt the Misfit puts on, but right now she feels love for him and for the whole Creation.

One may find this transformation too radical, if not strangely contrived, in any case less probable than the transformations undergone by the protagonists of the other stories. This sudden metamorphosis might be a way to soften the cruel but just punishment of the horrible grandmother. You must try to develop your own interpretation as well. The very last dialogue between Bobby Lee and the Misfit smacks of the terse humorous exchanges over fire shots in a *film noir* or a western, once justice has been done, but sadly again justice seems to be able to work only through extreme violence.

5

The devil and the problem of evil

Evil

Flannery O'Connor's feels the presence of evil everywhere. It is not just a Catholic obsession, but rather a constant preoccupation of all Christians, and quite strongly then of American Protestants as well. Most of American literature has always dealt with this issue.

Though the stories are set in the South of the USA, Flannery O'Connor extends her references to the whole world: there are several strong allusions to Europe (in "A Good Man Is Hard to Find", "The Displaced Person"), to the Jews ("A Temple of the Holy Ghost").

Evil has several guises: self-complacency, jealousy, all the sins that could be listed in a catechism book. More importantly it is expressed in the negation of God, as exemplified in Hulga's over strict rationalism, and also in the worship of something else than God.

"The Catholic novelist believes that you destroy your freedom by sin; the modern reader believes, I think, that you gain it in that way." (Flannery O'Connor, "In the Devil's Territory", 1961, *in* Ellsberg, 127-8)

The Devil

The word "devil" is recurrent in Flannery O'Connor's fiction and essays. What does it mean for her? What is his dramatic function? What are his means of seduction?

The meaning of the devil

The Devil is the particular way the Christians account for evil in the world. Other cultures have devised other stratagems to explain it. Flannery O'Connor adheres to the Catholic dogma which holds that a devil is a fallen angel, an actual being present in the world and whose mission it is to divert us from God. It is not a psychological trend of our minds. Flannery O'Connor likes to quote Baudelaire's « La plus grande ruse du diable est de nous faire croire qu'il n'existe pas. »

One passage illustrates this perfectly well. In "The Displaced Person" Mrs Shortley exclaims: "I would suspicion salvation got from the devil," and further down, the narrative voice continues with her inner thoughts: "She had never given much thought to the devil for she felt that religion was essentially for those people who didn't have the brains to avoid evil without it [...] if she had given it much thought, she would have considered the devil the head of it and God the hanger-on." The narrative voice (the author's?) insidiously goes on: "With the coming of these displaced people, she was obliged to give new thoughts to a good many things". (203-204) The latter remark implies on the literal level: how to lodge them, pay them, etc., but on another level it means that their intrusion into a settled life challenges the previous vision she had on religion and on salvation.

Once he has accepted the actual existence of the devil, the Christian must fight against him and remain aware that one of his tricks consists in transferring one's fear of him onto someone else or something: the Displaced Person is feared for no reason.

The devil's dramatic function

He never triumphs over God, he loses the fight just as he is on the point of winning the soul of his victims. His actions help create the dramatic situations that will allow grace to act upon the victims. The forces of good and evil collide violently within mostly strong-headed characters. God rescues His creatures at the point of no return where the devil had cornered them. These are the moments of revelation and redemption we have already analyzed.

The dramatic function of the devil is clearly explained by its creator:

> In my stories a reader will find that the devil accomplishes a good deal of groundwork that seems to be necessary before grace is effective... To insure our sense of mystery, we need a sense of evil which sees the devil as a real spirit who must be made to name himself with his specific personality for every occasion [...] The novelist can no longer reflect a balance from the world he sees around him; instead, he has to try to create one [...] When such a writer has a freak for his hero, he is not simply showing us what we are, but what we have been and what we could become. His prophet-freak is an image of himself [...] From my own experience in trying to make stories 'work', I have discovered that what is needed is an action that is totally unexpected, yet totally believable, and I have found that, for me, this is always an action which indicates that grace has been offered. And frequently it is an action in which the devil has been the unwilling instrument of grace. ("In the Devil's Territory", 1961, *in* Ellsberg, 128)

The devil's means of seduction

They can be grouped in a trinity of traps: the attraction for material things (money, coca-cola, cars, sex), pride, secular autonomy...

The attraction for material artifacts characterizes our society

The 1950's saw the tremendous social changes brought about by prosperity, uncannily due to the war, evil incarnate. It was also the Cold War and the period of McCarthysm. "The American Way of Life" was elevated to the rank of a real divinity, overpowering all other ways of life, and in the process replacing the one and only true God for the decades to come. The Catholic writer condemns the adoration of the new golden calves to which people sacrifice their freedom and their labor. Materialism forces the expectations of people away from the transcendent, away from the word of God, towards false gods, like those the Hebrews turned to in the desert once Moses had left them to seek God's commandments. O'Connor strikes her erring characters as angrily as Moses when he came down the hill and saw his people had reverted to paganism under Aaron's helpless supervision. She maims them, plagues them like God in the Sinai, so that in blood they may repent and redirect their prayers away from the golden statues to God. The new pagan divinities have not changed much:

• The first, *money* is everywhere present in the stories, and as Mrs. McIntyre says "It is the root of all evil" (which of course does not keep her from being obsessed with it). In the same story we see how her safe (*coffre fort*) becomes her tabernacle, but one which is symbolically empty, hidden in a dark room which is the chapel of this pagan god: "she went into the black hall, a closet-like space that was dark and quiet as a chapel [...] Old banknotes and ledgers were stacked... and there was a small safe, empty but locked, set like a tabernacle in the center of it." (221)

• The second seduction is younger. It is supposed to quench thirst but can never quench spiritual thirst: *Coca-Cola.* In the days of O'Connor it was mostly famous in the South, but obviously she foresaw its global fame, a menace to the global true God. Its symbolism is most developed in "A Late Encounter with the Enemy". John Wesley stops by the Coca-Cola machine to freshen up and thus delays the entry of the grandfather onto the stage. Worse, at the end the boy wheels the dead man to join the queue, not to pass St Peter at the door of Paradise, but to reach the Coca-Cola machine...: "That crafty scout had bumped him out the back way and rolled him at high speed down a flagstone path and was waiting now, with the corpse, in the long line at the Coca-Cola machine." (144) By then we will have noticed that the founder of Methodism is a true devil: he has his "blouse loose behind", forming thus a tail, "his hip and cheek pressed to the red machine" (141), the color red being that of the devil (when it is not that of Christ's blood).

• *Machines.* The machine that distributes pagan fluids echoes the machine in "The Artificial Nigger", to which the grandfather and the boy ask for their horoscope and weight, as if, once more, they could fathom the future and the whole truth about themselves. As we know it makes mistakes, because it is just a machine, but they want to believe the machine makes only minor mistakes. Machines are the product of man's uncontainable thirst for power: through his making them, man can feel he has equated the Creator.

In her dislike for machines, Flannery O'Connor somehow joins the long series of American writers who see in technology the destruction of the pristine wilderness bequeathed pure by God to the Americans. The train that snakes around the woods to take Mr. Head and Nelson to the city and back stands for the iron avatar of Satan in the Garden of Eden, and it echoes the train that rapes the deep woods of *Go Down, Moses*, by William Faulkner.

The modern golden calf is of course the *car,* far more frequent in the stories than the train. We have already seen several of its functions in the quest for redemption. It is otherwise (and often at the same time) the focus of envy. The best story for this development is "The Life You Save May Be Your Own". Shiftlet is attracted to the car and only remains on the farm until he can get it. He becomes the epitome of the damned. Yet, as always in Flannery O'Connor's fiction, the symbol is multiple. His arrival transforms the life of the two women and as he fidgets with the engine of the car he also fidgets with the brain of Lucynell who becomes able then to pronounce the first word of her life: "bird", which can be read as "spirit".

Shiflet echoes Hazel Motes who exclaims in *Wise Blood*: "Nobody with a good car needs to be justified". A common word in the Bible Belt, "justified" here means specifically to be saved by God. Obviously Shiftlet transforms the car into an idol, much as Hulga does with her leg. "For him it is not just a car but the image of his driven self; he sees it as an emblem of disincarnated spirit: 'the spirit is like a car.' [...] [he] commits the idolatrous act of imposing a transcendent significance on the car and ignoring its concrete reality [...] there is no change in his vision of things or their meaning, no revelation of mystery". (Desmond 48-9)

However the end of this quote is open to discussion, for the car does take Shiftlet to Mobile. Grant it, it is a city whose name contradicts the immobility a city is supposed to stand for, but perhaps Shiftlet will set his eyes afterwards not just on the "bumper that glittered in the distance" but on the lights of God glittering somewhere in the distance beyond. The ending is also very reminiscent of that of *The Violent Bear It Away*, in which the self-proclaimed prophet slouches "toward the dark city where the children of God lay sleeping"; again an ambiguous ending, which probably implies his future prophesying there, but also perhaps his burning "the children of God" or drowning them as we have already seen him do.

As we have seen for the grandmother of "A Good Man Is Hard to Find", cars can also allow for the initiation of characters, since they are the vehicle of their quest. The train the grandfather takes with his grandson in "The Artificial Nigger" performs a similar dual function: we have seen that it is first a snake of iron penetrating the countryside, and like the snake in the Garden of Eden, it offers the characters the possibility to reach knowledge, through disobedience. Nonetheless, it is thanks to their trip that the two characters can be initiated into the mystery of love and grace. The train as snake supports their sinful pride in the beginning but then helps them see the light and delivers them back safely to their home, "trans-formed".

• *Gambling, sex and drinking,* "offerings at the shrine of a goddess" (289) are well-known traps set by the devil. They are not fully developed in the stories and only appear in "Good Country", in a manner forceful enough however to mark the reader's mind. Sex is far more present in *Wise Blood* than it is here in the short stories.

Pride

Most protagonists are self-righteous; ambitious, envious. Hyman uses the term "self-intoxicated". This seems to be mostly the case of female characters, typically widows and in particular those who own farmland (Mrs. Cope, Mrs. McIntyre), or also younger ones like Hulga, but several male characters share this major fault: Mr. Head, and his grand-son, Mr. Shortley…

Vanity implies the refusal of the other, of the other's values by highly considering one's own. The devil can also lead people into being exactly the contrary, that is to say to be never satisfied, never able to accept themselves as they are. Defeating the devil will imply accepting oneself. Ruby is such a character ("A Stroke of Good Fortune"), as well as the child in "A Temple of the Holy Ghost". These characters are believers in the "gospel of scorn" (Thomas Merton) that they address to themselves and to God. Flannery O'Connor's role is to make them turn to the real gospel of love for all of God's creation, themselves included.

Secular autonomy

In the West the concept of the death of God has developed in conjunction with the quest for material happiness. Intellectuals have in great numbers forsaken theology to turn instead to the different sciences. Flannery O'Connor herself had studied social sciences at the university and had hated them.

• *Science.* Mrs. Hopewell ("Good Country") reads one of her daughter's books: "Science, on the other hand, has to assert its soberness and seriousness afresh and declare that it is concerned solely with what-is." (277) Immediately, Mrs. Hopewell senses the devil behind the book: "These words […] worked on Mrs. Hopewell like some evil incantation in gibberish. She shut the book quickly and went out of the room as if she were having a chill." (277) In fact she is feeling the wind made by the devil, a well-known property of witches as well!

Hulga is convinced her PhD has allowed her to see through the Christian lie. In reality she will need to lose her glasses to be able to understand the mystery of life. That she should have a weak heart (like the salesman) is highly symbolic of her lacking love and understanding.

Hulga's predicament is the perfect example of how the devil entices people to transfer their sense of value from the essential to a material thing. Let us stop at how Flannery O'Connor builds her demonstration.

• *The wooden leg.* Flannery O'Connor commented herself on the image of the wooden leg:

> The average reader is pleased to observe anybody's wooden leg being stolen. But without ceasing to appeal to him and without making any statement of high intention, this story does manage to operate at another level of experience, by letting the wooden leg accumulate meaning. Early in the story, we're presented with the fact that the PhD. Is spiritually as well as physically crippled. She believes in nothing but her own belief in nothing, and we perceive that there is a wooden part of her soul that corresponds to the wooden leg. Now of course this is never stated. The fiction writer states as little as possible. The reader makes this connection from things he is shown. He may not even know that he makes the connection, but the connection is there nevertheless and it has its effect on him. As the story goes on, the wooden leg continues to accumulate meaning. The reader learns how the girl feels about her leg, how her mother feels about it, and how the country woman on the place feels about it; and finally, by the time the Bible salesman comes along, the leg has accumulated so much meaning that it is, as the saying goes, loaded. And when the Bible salesman steals it, the reader realizes that he has taken away part of the girl's personality and has revealed her deep affliction to her for the first time.
>
> If you want to say that the wooden leg is a symbol, you can say that. But it is a wooden leg first, and as a wooden leg it is absolutely necessary to the story. It has its place on the literal level of the story, but it operates in depth as well as on the surface. It increases the story in every direction, and this is essentially the way a story escapes being short. (*Mystery and Manners* 98-100)

Hulga has a skewed vision because: "she has elevated her leg to the status of an idol […] she has made an idol of herself, signified by the act of renaming herself […]. To view the leg and herself as Hulga does involves an act of metaphysical displacement, a gnostic refusal to see the object and herself as they really are. Therefore, Manley Pointer's theft [...] is in fact a destruction of the false idol. [It] precipitates an incarnational movement, leaving Hulga at least open to a new way of seeing things — most important, of seeing herself as a confounded, contradictory, yet mysterious human creature [...] [It] has in fact made Hulga potentially free." (Desmond 44)

How does the devil concretely appear in the narration?

His description corresponds to that of the Catholic iconography: a real man (Flannery O'Connor wrote before gender-inclusive characters became a politically correct obligation in publications!) with red flesh, a tail, etc.

His dramatic function is conveyed through direct catalysts (of these devilish-turned-divine dramas) that are always physical persons, or the reproduction of one (the artificial nigger). These can be angelic people (Mr. Guizac), grotesques, avatars of the devil.

These avatars often come in devilish trinities (probably to mock the divine one) and they all look alike, so that they really are three in one or one in three. They often turn red.

– The Misfit is helped by two acolytes. His eyes are red rimmed (132).

– There are three nasty boys in "The River": "on the porch there were three little boys of different sizes with identical speckled faces." (160)

– and in "A Circle of Fire" as well: "The three boys looked something alike except that the middle one" wore glasses. (178)

The three boys in "The River" torture Bevel by having him rolled over by the pigs. Now we know the pigs contain the evil spirits expelled from the possessed man by Jesus. The hog hurts Bevel but cannot kill him. Also, one of the Misfit's friends disgusted June Star because he reminded her of a pig. (131)

In "A Circle of Fire" the three boys are real devils. One wears a destroyer on his shirt. He then removes it and sticks it in the back of his trousers like a tail, exactly like John Wesley fusing into the red Coca-Cola machine. The three devils let loose the bull, defying the property instinct of Mrs. Cope and liberating brutal natural strength. We then realize that this liberation is, like that of the pigs, the necessary condition for the conversion of the lady who until then was a prisoner of her material possessions, much like Hulga with her leg. We grasp the meaning of the devils as harbingers of grace and we remember that they had "white penetrating stares" and that "Powell's stare seemed to pinch her like a pair of tongs." These instruments of torture turn into forceps to deliver her from evil ("Deliver us from evil" is one line of the Christian prayer *Our Father*).

Flannery O'Connor goes as far as transforming these freaks into prophets, into those Old Testament heroes who had perished in the fire for not having renounced their faith. Though some readers have criticized this last stroke as being too farfetched, it allows us to comprehend the duality of the dramatic function of the devil: without him grace would not be necessary and thus not possible.

Thus the protagonists can be said to sign with the devil a pact that opens for them the door to a satanic experience, to the reality of evil which immediately forces them to become aware of their spiritual needs. This is the Faustian dilemma. The devil is the dragon one must fear and avoid being eaten by, but which we must necessarily pass by, for there cannot be an initiation into good if one has not been at least grazed by evil.

6

Anagogy in Flannery O'Connor's fiction: an analysis of "A Temple of The Holy Ghost"

This story may sometimes appear as too hermetic at first sight, but it is fairly easy to decode.

An analysis of the final passage

Take the end of the story from "You'd think she had to catch a train" (247). In *Risen Sons* John Desmond notes the fidelity of Flannery O'Connor to the literal details of the scene, to "*observed* reality." As the scene unfolds we discover the little girl's change of mood and her linking up mentally the Elevation (of the Catholic mass), the hermaphrodite she heard about from Susan and Joanne, and human grotesqueness.

> Within that same movement, evoked through it analogically, we have an image of the historical Christian Incarnation, the Host, united to nature in the form of a hierophany, the Host-like sun 'drenched in blood' as it sets beyond the treeline... the action moves forward to dramatize meaning... there is a dynamic of reciprocal insight operating on two levels. One reads the words and the literal action (the movement of the child's mind) is both 'same' and 'different' from the historical analogue (the movement or incarnation of the divine into the things of this world)... O'Connor creates vision implicitly through the details of the passage—the Host, the freak, the nun's crucifix, Alonzo's pig ears, the sun, the trees. O'Connor preserves the

> mystery of the scene by leaving it to the reader to envision the 'connection' between the literal details and the hierophany, and she thereby respects both the created fictional world *and* the reader. (Desmond 22-24)

Let us look closely at the passage. The narrative voice makes it clear that it is during the "*Tantum Ergo*" (these words introduce the elevation: "*Tantum Ergo sacramentum...*". The whole text is sung in Latin by the cousins a few pages earlier[1]) that "her ugly thoughts stopped and she began to realize that she was in the presence of God" (247). She starts mechanically to pray and say the things she has been taught to say, but they still have an impact on her as even prayers learnt by heart can have. Then the elevated Host brings her to recall the freak. Just as the Host (*hostie*) is the mark of Jesus' acceptance of His fate, the child remembers the freaks's words her cousins reported to her at night, words that have haunted her since: "God made me thisaway and if you laugh..." (245) Here again she hears the freak accept his fate: "I don't dispute hit. This is the way He wanted me to be." (248)

This sudden realization is further imprinted onto the child, not just mentally but now physically, when the nun plays with her, embracing her tenderly and firmly, thereby "mashing the side of her face into the crucifix." (248) Christ's incarnation is not simply historical or theological: the author makes it clear that He is incarnated into the flesh of the child, who is but a surrogate for mankind.

The next lines typically refer to a journey, however short it may be, and the return home, which is the structure Flannery O'Connor chose to express the sense of mission and of understanding of her characters in all her works. One may also note that the two women are still sitting in the back of the car (earlier the child had sat in the front). This may be a sign of their not having reached full initiation into the mystery of Creation yet, which will be fulfilled for the child a little while later (we will come back to this). Or does it mean that they are being mockingly beaued around by Alonzo, in a reversal of the trick the little girl wanted to play on her cousins? Or simply that

1 French translation: Bénédiction du Saint-Sacrement, "*Tantum Ergo sacramentum...*": « Voilà le grand sacrement ; /Adorons-le, humblement prosternés/ Que l'antique loi/ Cède à la loi nouvelle !/ Que notre foi supplée /Aux défaillances de nos sens !/ Au Père et au Fils, / Louange et chant d'allégresse ; / Salut, honneur, puissance » (fin de l'extrait donné par FC) ; la suite est celle-ci : « Actions de grâces à jamais ! / À l'Esprit qui procède des deux, / Gloire et louange égales ! Ainsi soit-il, / Vous leur avez donné un pain du ciel. / Un pain qui renferme toutes les délices ». (Traduction tirée du *Paroissien romain*, de H. Dessain, Malines, 1922.)

they belong where they should, that is to say in a car driven by a chauffeur, which would imply that things have settled down with a now deeper understanding of the hidden values of the divine?

The remaining paragraphs will conclude this initiation for the little girl. The driver's neck and ears remind her of a pig, that is to say recall the freak at the fair, whom the man saw, even though he does not say it specifically, perhaps because he accepted it as a normal phenomenon. The child will not miss the freak since she will always have Alonzo's ears to perform the same function: this man probably accepts his ears, meant by God to be like this. There has been some progress too since, in the opening pages, Alonzo was described as being horribly fat and sweaty (238), whereas we now only see his ears! The child had then precisely used his ugliness to annoy the girls since she wanted him to escort, or "beau around" her cousins.

We must not forget either that the child is herself somewhat of a freak since she is fat and wears braces (the narrator's description of her in the opening pages, as she makes fun of her two idiotic cousins, is as pitiless as the child is towards her relatives). She thus belongs to a fraternity with the hermaphrodite and Alonzo, and we guess she comes to accept her own deformity along with them. We must notice that the "fat cheeks" she displayed in the opening pages have now become a pleasant "round face" which is but the reproduction in human form of the sun and Host.

One can also find another meaning in these pig's ears. Pigs are linked to the devil's work: the pigsty in "The River" clearly alludes to the story of the Gadarenes man possessed by evil spirits. Jesus "commanded the unclean spirits to come out of the man" and he made them enter nearby swine, "and the herd ran violently down a steep place into the lake, and were choked." (Luke 8: 26-39, also in Matthew 8: 28-34 and Mark 5: 1-20)

One could imagine that the little girl is the prisoner of the devil: he is driving the car, also an double-edged prop that is often negative in Flannery O'Connor's fiction for, as an object of envy, it has replaced the search for the holy. In "The Life You Save May Be Your Own", the car is for Shiftlet the golden calf. Also, it encloses people and shuts them from the actual and natural Creation. Similarly, the car of Mr. Cheatam had been likened to "the last circle in hell" by the child's mother in the beginning (239). In this respect, it is significant that it is only when she looks *through* the window and thus escapes the enclosed space of the car, that the child is overwhelmed by her vision of the sun as Host and God.

Yet, cars are also positive for they allow for displacement and discovery, and they can be seen as the modern day horses of medieval pilgrims. Calling the man's car "the last circle in hell" immediately evokes Dante's *Commedia*, a strong influence on O'Connor. Dante spoke himself of the different layers of meaning in a literary text and underlined the anagogical one.[1] The child is thus likened to Dante's pilgrims.

The last paragraph consecrates the full initiation of the little girl. She reaches it by looking though the glass of the window, that is through her reaching beyond the walls of her personal universe, in the platonician sense. Here again the treeline is of paramount importance since it signals the barrier between two worlds, which will fuse into one for the girl, even if she cannot have access to the full knowledge of the world beyond. The sun is itself the Host, and its light is the blood of Christ, shed for the atonement of sins, and for leading people on the right path, "the red clay road". In the sun are collapsed the flesh and blood of Christ, his whole incarnation, and not just one element of it. The sun is omnipresent in the story to represent God, just as the Holy Host is Christ, in reminiscence of old solar cults incorporated into Christianity.

Retracing our steps to the foundations of the Temple

To understand how Flannery O'Connor built the story from the very beginning to this epiphany, we must discover the clues she has sown

1 In a letter attributed to him, he explains to his sponsor Can Grande della Scalla that the Commedia "is not simple, but on the contrary can be called polysemous, that is to say "of more senses than one"...and the first is called literal, but the second allegorical or mystic. And this mode of treatment, for its better manifestation, may be considered in this verse: "When Israel came out of Egypt, and the house of Jacob from a people of strange speech, Judaea became his sanctification, Israel his power." For if we inspect the letter alone, the departure of the children of Israel out of Egypt in the time of Moses is presented to us; if the allegory, our redemption brought by Christ; if the moral sense, the conversion of the soul from the grief and misery of sin to the state of grace is presented to us; if the anagogical, the departure of the soul from the slavery of this corruption to the liberty of eternal glory is presented to us." (*in* Singleton 86-87)

on the way. These will tell us that from the start the child was highly perceptive of the sacred, even though she was unable to articulate it.

First clues: hyper sensitivity to things holy

We sense the girl's alertness to things holy when she strangely reacts to her cousins' explanation of their self-given names "Temple of the Holy Ghost". The cousins are laughing very hard but the child "didn't see anything so funny in this" (238) for she does not get the sexual innuendo the cousins perceive (profane level), but instead senses the reference to the divine presence in each human being (spiritual level). Her mother sides with her and is seen throughout the story as rather more perceptive and gentle than the other mothers of Flannery O'Connor's fiction.

From then on the child christens herself "Temple of the Holy Ghost" (238), and as she is never named otherwise in the text she becomes emblematic of children's purity, though, in another delightful perversion of what could pass for a manichean opposition between purity and sin, she remains pretty mean towards her entourage. However, she is fully conscious of this and asks God to "Hep me not to be so mean" in the end (247) (the reader feels she won't be able to improve on that point because it is such an intrinsic part of her self, but didn't "God made her thisaway"?). Hers is but one of the sins the story plays with: lust, lack of respect for the Lord's day that has been turned into a time of leisure (the text opens on "All weekend"), pride, self-righteousness...

The next episode involves the boys she has chosen to escort the girls: she described them as handsome and tall whereas they are short and monkey-like. What's more, when the girls expected to be courted, they find out that the boys can only sing respectful religious hymns. The scene turns burlesque with the girls singing in Latin. Yet what they sing heralds the redeeming moment of the end when the little girl realizes she is in contact with God during elevation, since the cousins sing the "*Tantum ergo...*" (241)

The sacred thus points under the comical. The scene becomes even more hilarious when the boys, who do not know Latin, exclaim: "That must be Jew singing" (241). Beyond the surface anti-semitism of these hillbillies, there is truth: the words are those that the Eucharist or the offering of a Jew's life for the redemption of sinners perform over and over again, it is thus indeed "Jew singing"!

The beacon light and the freak: Revelation

Another clue is the beacon light of the fair. The lexicon constantly revolves around light and darkness. When she remains alone in her room that she likes to be dark (a remark which underlines once more the separatedness she still suffers from at that stage), the child sees the light, hears the sound of the calliope, and has a vision in her head of the fair. She is constantly described with verbs of perception and thus as very sensitive to outside events and on the alert: "watch", "observe", "see", "hear", "thought", "reflected", "glare"...

To a child like her the fair is both fun and mystery since the time she went she was not supposed to see everything: "Certain tents were closed then because they contained things that would be known only to grown people". (242) The fair functions as a microcosm of Creation, but also as an echo of the Roman circuses where martyrs were mass-produced. She fantasizes about being a saint or a martyr (243), and even though, once more, it is narrated in a humorous way, such a desire reaches deep into the sacred. In a similar vein, her prayers and the way they develop show that even if they are perfunctory, she still devotes her full attention to them (she gets up from bed to kneel and pray when she realizes she has forgotten to say them) and with fervor visualizes the Crucifixion.

The scene in which she hears about the freak echoes those in which man yearns to learn about something that has been kept secret because there are things the human mind cannot fathom. One thinks of Adam and Eve's desperately wanting to possess knowledge, of Faust, Prometheus, etc. Here the child cannot understand how there could be a man who is also a woman with only one head. She is someone constantly using her own head/mind to outsmart people, but there are mysteries that she cannot figure out. Flannery O'Connor uses this prop (the hermaphrodite) to suggest there are mysteries God wants us to respect, and that there are areas we must not trespass for God severely punishes our transgressions (Adam and Eve...). "The Artificial Nigger" functions in the same way: the statue confronts Mr. Head, the equivalent in old age of the child here, to the mystery of evil and of grace.

Interestingly the freak's tent is "divided into two parts by a black curtain, one side for men and one for women." (245) If that is, on the *literal* level, because the hermaphrodite shows his underdress to the women only and his pants to the men only, we must continue our interpretation. The black curtain *allegorically* evokes the veil in the temple in Jerusalem (the temple is the center of the story, meaning the house of God which everyone of us is, according to Christianity, with also a reference to the most famous temple of the Bible), a veil which separated the ordinary people from the altar where only the empowered priests were allowed to go, a separation metaphorically representing the one between mankind and God. The stage division in the tent performs the same function: neither the men nor the women can encompass the hermaphrodite as a whole. *Anagogically*, this freak is an incarnation of God on earth, something holy, someone like Jesus who accepts His fate, but also something unfathomable and forever mysterious.. It can only be comprehended through faith, not through the intellect, or the head, as the child desperately tries to. It is when she stops trying to put things straight and lets her mind fuse visions that she reaches understanding.

Flannery O'Connor continues weaving together the child's intuition of the sacred and her impossibility to master everything by granting her the vision of herself combining the freak's acceptance of his freakness and her being a temple of the Holy Ghost. It is almost the final stage in her initiation, but she needs more prompting and this is why the author has her go to sleep at that point, to restore her strength (246).

When the next day she rides in the front of the car we can read a clue here as to her having received knowledge, as having passed from the back to the front in the classroom. Again it is a freakish detail that allows her to be in contact with the mystery of the sun as Host: the driver stinks and she has to hold her head *out* the window. This allows her to "look directly into the ivory sun" (top of page 247). She is thus looking at the glory of God and this is confirmed down the page when "the priest raised the monstrance with the Host shining ivory-colored". Earlier on the sun had been "framed in the middle of the blue afternoon" just as now the Host was shining "in the center of" the monstrance (247-8).

Such a Revelation, in the spiritual sense of the word, had been announced in the material world early in the story during the dinner the mother had prepared for the cousins: "she had a table laid out there under some Japanese lanterns". The child refuses to participate in the celebration out of pride for she thinks too highly of herself and does not want to mix with idiots. Yet, from the kitchen she cannot help looking: "The lanterns gilded the leaves of the trees orange… and above them was black-green and below them were different dim muted colors that made the girls sitting at the table look prettier than they were" (242), something of course the child cannot accept. *Literally*, the lanterns give out different hues, thereby separating the scene into opposite layers of light and darkness. *Metaphorically*, this reproduces the different levels of understanding in the child's soul (darkness and light), but also contains the very same colors as in the last paragraph (red and black-green), thus, *anagogically* heralding the glorious sun/God setting over "a gathering greenness until it touched the dark woods." (248)

Red: color and sacrifice

The color red permeates the whole story. In the first lines it is said that the two girls removed their convent uniforms to put on red skirts and loud blouses. Furthermore one has red hair and the other "turns purple in patches" when she laughs (236). Their profane clothes, their lipstick and their being partly red physically evoke their lust and basely sinful nature. The boys and various characters are also portrayed as being red. This links them to the devil, or to dragons that the little girl has to encounter before she can triumph over them. The red at the very end of the story shows that a long initiation into the Good has been achieved: it is the red of the sun, of the blood of God and of the good road the faithful will follow to be with God. Again here the color has led the readers from the literal level: lipstick, red face of White southerners burnt by the sun, the glowing sun…, to the allegorical: lust, love, sex, fires of all sorts, to the anagogical: the blood of Christ and through it the redemption of sinners.

The convent

It is a powerful place that frames the story entirely: right in the beginning the cousins come out of it and the child goes there with them at the end. It is a Catholic stronghold of a sort in a profane environment: it is located in the middle of town. The filling station on one side belongs to the pagan world of cars. On the other side, the firehouse is meant to extinguish fires. This can be felt as being reassuring, but it can also be seen as something dangerous in the economy of Flannery O'Connor's fiction. Fires are very frequent in her stories: self-proclaimed prophets typically set fire to houses and farms: *The Violent Bear it Away*, "A Circle in the Fire"… It is hard to say whether their setting things on fire proceeds from the devil or from God. The epigraph from St Cyril of Jerusalem that is printed in the opening pages of some editions of *A Good Man is Hard to Find* warns us that we must beware of the trials on our path: "The dragon is by the side of the road, watching those who pass. Beware lest he devour you. We go to the father of souls, but it is necessary to pass by the dragon." The fires in the stories are those spat by the dragons in an act of cleansing, and trying to put them out through the recourse to a fire brigade may be seen as another proof of human stupid and useless hubris.

The convent operates here as a sort of trap (the child is very suspicious: "You put your foot in their door and they got you praying", 247) forcing the child to come to terms with the holy, and finally releasing her once she has reached the final stages of her initiation. Even though it is of course motionless, the convent is likened to the trains or cars most protagonists have to take on their way to enlightenment, as we saw earlier. Indeed, as the nun has the little group hurry down the corridor, the child feels: "You'd think she has to catch a train" (247).

We must also remember that the convent is called Mount St. Scholastica (the name is given on the 6th line of the story, it is thus a very early clue). This is an obvious reference to the school of thought of the same name (Scholastics) that originally developed in the Middle Ages, particular the XIIIth century. Its theologians developed methods to analyze and interpret texts which are at the origin of our own methods of interpretation and "commentaire de texte" (lectio, quaestio, disputatio). This is again from the part of the author an allusion to the need to perceive the different layers of meaning in a text.

The conflict between Catholicism and Protestantism

The convent is not simply surrounded by the secular space of the city, it is an island in the middle of a Protestant culture. We have seen that Flannery O'Connor did admire the passion and zeal with which the Baptist preachers constantly plied their trade, but she reproached them with their shortsightedness regarding the mystery of Incarnation and Redemption. The convent can be seen as representing an intrusion for those Protestants, and this may be why they have placed the fire brigade next to it, so as to put out the spiritual fire emanating from it…

The Virgin Mary is also included in this highly Catholic story through the name of the city where the convent stands: Mayville. In the South, as we know, a lot of place names end in *ville* in replacement of *town* to thank the French after the war of independence. However, the name was coined with a purpose here: the suffix refers to France and to its Catholic culture and Catholic thinkers to whom O'Connor was very close (Pierre Teilhard de Chardin, Jacques Maritain, François Mauriac notably). As for May, it is the month of Mary.

Many O'Connor's stories make fun of various Protestant idiosyncrasies, but here the mockery is particularly vitriolic. Several denominations are ironically alluded to. Miss Kirkby evokes Presbyterianism with the word *kirk*, Scottish for *church,* in her name. The hilarious description of this spinster who "blushed and carried her fork delicately to her mouth with one pea on it" conveys the prudishness and miserliness commonly associated with the Calvinistic Scotch-Irish who settled in the South, whereas O'Connor was of Catholic Irish stock.

Another victim of the little girl's irony is the Church of God, to whom the boys are supposed to belong. It is a denomination deriving from Baptism and close to Pentecostalism. The child declares to her cousins, as if she were a very learned adult: "Somebody said they were both going to be Church of God preachers because you don't have to know nothing to be one." (239) And of course, when the boys are startled by the Latin sung by the cousins and Wendell begins to tune his guitar, she calls him "You big dumb Church of God ox!" (241)

This emphasis on the fact that you don't have to know much to be a preacher points to one of the major differences between the two branches of Christianity, namely the radically opposite importance of the clergy for the congregations. In Protestantism, the individual believer is in direct contact with God, through the Bible, and in its most popular forms in the South anybody can become a preacher without any theological training. The minister or preacher is not a go-between, he is just there to maintain a certain level of religious practice and teaching.

The blindfolds of the Southern preachers are shown in the reference to their incapacity to accept the fair and all it encompasses. Alonzo reports that the preachers who inspected the fair had it closed down for good. Knowing what Flannery O'Connor thinks of Evangelists, this can only mean that they did not have the proper vision of the Creation and found the freak disturbing whereas they should have understood its function in the divine design.

In Catholicism on the contrary, the clergy is radically separated from his congregation, both in terms of daily life as he must remain celibate, and in terms of intellectual and theological training. For someone like O'Connor, this intense meditation is required to reach the transcendent, and above all to bring ordinary human beings towards an understanding of it. The priest is, on the human plane, the equivalent of Christ: he is a mediator between the two orders of life, the material, the lowly and the transcendent, just as a writer like O'Connor, or Dante and many others for that matter, are mediators, leading their readers from the mundane to the anagogical.

This necessity is illustrated by a seemingly banal sentence, highly polysemous once more. When she is in the car going to the convent at the end, as we have already seen, the child holds her head out the window: "With her hair blowing into her face she could look directly into the ivory sun which was framed in the middle of the blue afternoon but when she pulled it away from her eyes she had to squint." (247) *Literally*, her hair gets into her face and nicely shades her eyes from the burning sun, but *anagogically* this refers to the Catholic priesthood and mediation: if you look directly at the sun/God, as the Protestants do, you "squint", you do not get the proper vision, it is distorted, and you burn your eyes. If you have a mediator, a guide, you can look into the ivory sun/God without any hindrance or damage.

Conclusion

The structure of "A Temple of the Holy Ghost" follows the anagogical movement explained above, that is to say a movement of elevation, from the ludicrous scenes of the beginning with the child literally rolling on the floor (237) when she laughs so hard at her own good jokes that she convulses and falls from her chair, to her being "level" with the floor ("The child was standing on a barrel pushed into some bushes at the side of the house, her face level with porch floor", 240), to her dignified position in the car at the end with her head elevated to the sky and the sun, after having attended the Elevation during mass.

This upward movement towards salvation has implied encountering and triumphing over the many traps the devil has dropped on the child's path: lust, stupidity, self-righteousness, the desire to possess perfect knowledge, but the fascination for the holy carries the little girl to the highest point of human experience and transmutes red lipstick into the blood of atonement, vice into virtue, a weekend of leisure into the mass of Sun/Godday, ignorance into the acceptance of the holy mystery of Incarnation and Redemption.

7

A short general conclusion

Flannery O'Connor's books perfectly exemplify how a text can be read with multiple meanings and also prove, if need be, the overwhelming relevance of religion in American life until today. None of these stories has become outdated, and you can still find writers wrestling with the same subject matter nowadays. Few however have the cutting wit and extraordinary flair for the transcendent potentialities of the burlesque Flannery O'Connor possesses. We as readers stand pretty much like the little boy of "The River", lost and twisted, in the dark. I hope this course will be the helping though imperfect and spotted hand guiding you through the intricacies of Flannery O'Connor's symbolic journey, so that you can somehow be "fixed right" at Judgment Day!

> The child stood glum and limp in the middle of the dark living room while his father pulled him into a plaid coat. His right arm was hung in the sleeve but the father buttoned the coat anyway and pushed him forward toward a pale spotted hand that stuck through the half-open door.
> "He ain't fixed right", a loud voice said from the hall. (157)

Seconde partie

Cette seconde partie, portant sur l'ensemble des nouvelles, se concentrera sur des questions de formes : schémas récurrents, composition, images.
On s'attachera moins ici à prendre en compte la dimension religieuse des textes (sans toutefois la passer sous silence) qu'à sonder les richesses d'une écriture qui peut aussi procurer un plaisir de lecture à un public non croyant.

Marie-Claude Perrin-Chenour

8

Le sanctuaire dévoyé, topos du gothique sudiste

La grande maison patricienne qui a connu son heure de gloire, mais n'abrite plus que le mal, est une figure récurrente de la littérature du Sud des États-Unis. Lieu équivalent du château gothique des romans anglais du même nom, ce sanctuaire dévoyé prend souvent la forme d'une ancienne demeure de planteurs ruinés par la guerre de Sécession. Le péché originel, responsable de sa chute, est bien sûr l'institution de l'esclavage qui fait retour dans la conscience sudiste sous forme d'une lancinante culpabilité.

Bien avant la guerre, ce motif avait pourtant déjà été introduit dans la littérature du Sud par Edgar Allan Poe chez qui il se teintait d'accents puritains. C'est dans le conte intitulé « The Masque of the Red Death » qu'il trouve son expression la plus aboutie. Dans un pays et à une époque indéterminés, où la peste fait rage, un prince nommé Prospero décide de se barricader, avec quelques courtisans, dans un château gothique, espérant ainsi se protéger de la mort qui rode alentour. Dans sept salons décorés de couleurs différentes, les rescapés occupent leurs jours et leurs nuits à danser, à manger et à boire, tentant d'ignorer les tintements d'une grande horloge qui égrène les heures pour leur rappeler, contre leur gré, leur condition de mortels. Et ils parviennent en effet à s'étourdir suffisamment pour oublier le Temps qui passe. Aussi sont-ils d'autant plus surpris lorsqu'ils découvrent parmi eux un convive masqué dont le déguisement évoque la « peste rouge » et la mort. Voulant chasser l'intrus, ils le poursuivent jusque dans la dernière pièce (celle qui est tendue de tissu noir et ornée de vitraux rouge sang) pour s'apercevoir que son habit ne recouvre qu'une forme vide, car il est l'incarnation du néant qui s'ouvre devant eux au moment où tous tombent morts.

La mort à laquelle on essaie d'échapper pour découvrir qu'on la porte en soi est un thème commun à Poe et à Hawthorne. C'est toute la symbolique, par exemple, de « The Lily's Quest » ou de « The Birth Mark ». Mais, plus que la mort, ce qui hante l'univers de Poe, comme celui de Flannery O'Connor, c'est d'abord le Mal. Leurs personnages prétendent le tenir en respect, le maintenir hors de portée de leur univers clos, élaborer des stratégies de défense, pour se faire pourtant surprendre par lui au moment où ils s'y attendent le moins. Car le Mal arbore le visage du familier, voire de l'innocence. Il renverse les barrières patiemment érigées par les « braves gens » les plus prudents et, semble-t-il, les plus sages, pour s'installer au cœur de leur vie intime. Et leur maison, leur monde, leur corps même, conçus comme des sanctuaires inviolables, finissent par être envahis et minés de l'intérieur.

Sur le plan thématique cela se traduit par un schéma récurrent : celui de l'invasion d'un espace clos par un intrus. Sur le plan stylistique, cela explique l'abondance d'images de seuils, de barrières, de frontières, de lignes de démarcation. Ce schéma permet également la mise en place d'une dialectique intérieur/extérieur et d'une stratégie de renversement qui fonctionne tant verticalement qu'horizontalement.

La maison, espace protégé

Les personnages d'O'Connor sont tous repliés sur un univers limité qui fonctionne comme une extension d'eux-mêmes. Et s'aventurer hors de cette coquille ou de cette deuxième peau qu'ils se fabriquent pour se rassurer représente presque toujours un danger.

La maison doit s'entendre ici au sens large puisqu'il s'agit souvent d'une propriété plus ou moins grande, allant de la plantation du Sud *ante bellum* à l'appartement new-yorkais en passant par la ferme de taille moyenne symbolisant le Nouveau Sud de l'après guerre de Sécession.

Dans les fermes, la maison constitue généralement le point central, le poste d'observation du personnage focalisant le récit. Elle est entourée de plusieurs niveaux de clôtures, représentées par les barrières des différents champs, jardins, et prairies qui composent la propriété. À l'extrême limite de ces cercles concentriques, la ligne d'horizon est matérialisée par une forêt sombre qui arrête la vue et semble nier l'existence même d'un monde extérieur puisque seul le soleil (ou parfois la lune) peut se glisser derrière ce décor quasi immuable.

La nouvelle « A Circle in the Fire » met très clairement en place cette topographie faite de couches successives destinées à protéger la maison de l'intrusion du Mal. Le centre de conscience du récit est celui d'un personnage décrit par le narrateur comme « the child » (son nom, Sally Virginia, n'est mentionné qu'une seule fois). Puisque le lecteur est censé voir par ses yeux, la fillette n'est pas décrite – tout au moins jusqu'à trois pages avant la fin où la voix narrative prend le relais des observations de l'enfant. Pendant les trois quarts du récit donc, Sally Virginia est soit agenouillée sous l'une ou l'autre des fenêtres du premier étage de la maison d'où elle épie les conversations de sa mère, Mrs. Cope, avec son employée, Mrs. Pritchard, soit postée en haut de l'escalier d'où elle observe les deux mêmes femmes lorsqu'elles bavardent dans la cuisine. Son champ d'action est donc aussi restreint que son champ de vision puisque ce dernier est limité par l'encadrement de la fenêtre d'une part (« She was kneeling down by the window so that only her eyes and forehead showed over the sill », 180) et par la rampe de l'escalier d'autre part (« She got up and went out into the hall and leaned over the banisters. Mrs. Cope and Mrs. Pritchard's legs were facing each other in the back hall », 181). La maison, tout comme l'enfant, n'est pas décrite. En fait, réduite aux deux fenêtres par lesquelles la fillette voit les alentours et à la cuisine où elle prend ses repas avec sa mère, elle évoque un visage où se dessineraient deux yeux et une bouche et revêt ainsi une dimension anthropomorphique. Elle *est* la fillette elle-même dont la virginité (suggérée par son nom) doit être protégée du monde extérieur.

Lorsque le récit débute, Mrs. Cope est en train d'arracher les mauvaises herbes qui poussent autour de sa demeure. Elle s'active frénétiquement « as if [the weeds] were an *evil* sent directly by the *devil* to destroy the place » (175, c'est moi qui souligne). Sur le seuil, il faut donc éradiquer le Mal qui pourrait pénétrer à l'intérieur. Plus tard, il deviendra clair que le danger redouté ici est celui de la défloration de la jeune fille (Mrs. Cope ne voudra pas laisser entrer les garçons dans la maison – ceux-ci devront rester sur le pas de la porte – et refusera que sa fille aille leur parler à l'extérieur). Mais, au début, il peut aussi renvoyer à la mort qui obsède Mrs. Pritchard.

Cette dernière, debout sur la pelouse que Mrs. Cope s'évertue à « purifier » de ses mauvaises graines, ne peut s'empêcher de raconter des histoires morbides. Et les litanies lénifiantes de la propriétaire des lieux, qui tente désespérément de détourner la conversation, ne parviennent pas à endiguer le flot de ses mauvais présages. La phrase de Mrs. Pritchard, répétée plusieurs fois par la suite (« There ain't a thing you can do about it ») devient emblématique de cette situation originelle, elle-même symbolisant à l'évidence la chute de l'homme et la perte de l'innocence et du paradis. Pourtant, à ce stade, Mrs. Cope ignore que sa fille les écoute et croit encore celle-ci bien protégée à l'intérieur. D'autant plus que la topographie de la propriété semble en faire une forteresse inviolable mettant la jeune fille à l'abri comme une princesse dans sa tour :

> Sometimes the last line of trees was *a solid gray-blue wall* a little darker than the sky but this afternoon it was *almost black* and behind it the sky was a livid glaring white. (175) [...]
> The child thought the blank sky looked as if it were pushing against *the fortress wall*, trying to break through. (176) [...]
> [...] the child would scowl and not answer or glare up once across the lawn and two front pastures to *the gray-blue sentinel line of trees* (176) [...]
> *The fortress line of trees* was a granite blue. (190, c'est moi qui souligne)

Les termes « fortress » et « sentinel » renvoient au lexique du roman gothique avec son château bien gardé. La succession des barrières rappelle l'enfilade des salons de la maison maudite dans le conte de Poe, d'autant plus que la rangée d'arbres qui la clôt (comme la dernière salle du château) devient de plus en plus sombre au cours du récit pour se parer, à la fin, des teintes rouge sang du soleil couchant. Or, là aussi, un « villain » viendra souiller la pureté du sanctuaire et troubler l'harmonie qui y règne. En fait, cet intrus se présentera sous la forme de trois mauvais garçons – sorte de trinité inversée – dont le caractère diabolique sera révélé par leur rire méchant, lui-même répété trois fois :

> It was an evil laugh, full of calculated meanness, and she had heard it come three times, herself, distinctly. (190)

Chez Flannery O'Connor, les mauvaises actions réitérées trois fois évoquent les trois reniements du Christ par Pierre, ce qui laisse entrevoir un espoir de pardon et de rédemption pour les « villains ». Mais si, à la fin, les trois garçons peuvent en effet devenir, tels des « anges » ou des « prophètes », les agents d'une révélation de la misère du monde pour l'enfant et sa mère, pendant l'essentiel du récit, ils représentent d'abord et avant tout l'intrusion du Mal, la pénétration par effraction d'un élément étranger et dangereux dans un univers bien ordonné.

Dans cette nouvelle, comme dans d'autres, le combat du Bien contre le Mal est figuré par une lutte pour s'approprier un territoire. Et les stratégies de conquête sont identiques dans les deux camps. Pour Mrs. Cope, nous l'avons vu, il s'agit de construire un univers spatialement hiérarchisé qui s'organise en cercles de plus en plus larges autour du noyau central à protéger. Mais il est frappant de constater que « l'invasion » par les garçons de la ville de l'univers bucolique de la pastorale est représentée par la même métaphore d'encerclement. Les trois garçons sont identiques aux yeux des femmes de la maison et sont eux aussi hiérarchisés par rang de taille, sans doute pour être plus aisément classables et donc contrôlables. Ils possèdent le même regard dangereux (« All three boys had white penetrating stares », 179), bien que l'un d'entre eux semble plus menaçant dans la mesure où l'intensité de son regard est « redoublée » par le port de lunettes. Mais, ce qui le distingue avant tout (en dehors de l'image du « destroyer » qu'il arbore sur son sweat shirt et de son nom – Powell – qui, à une consonne près, évoque la puissance), c'est sa vision divergente qui donne l'impression qu'il peut « encercler » son adversaire et le maintenir en son pouvoir :

> One of his eyes had a slight cast to it so that his gaze seemed to be coming from two directions at once as if it had them *surrounded*. (178-179) [...]
> One of Powell's eyes seemed to be making *a circle of the place*, examining the house and the white water tower behind it and the chicken houses and the pastures that rolled away on either side *until they met the first line of woods*. (179) [...]
> Powell sat down on the edge of one of the chairs and looked as if he were trying to enclose the whole place in one *encircling* stare. (181, c'est moi qui souligne)

Comme on le voit dans la deuxième citation, le regard de Powell ne se contente pas de prendre son objet d'attention en étau (« Powell's stare seemed to pinch her like a pair of tongs », 180), il parcourt tout le territoire possédé par Mrs Cope en suivant la même gradation spatiale, semblant ainsi s'approprier chaque élément de son univers l'un après l'autre. Ainsi Powell devient-il le centre d'un cercle maléfique qui entre en compétition avec celui de Mrs. Cope et vise à le supplanter. Et sa victoire sera totale lorsqu'il sera parvenu à faire sortir la fillette de son poste d'observation, lui dérobant son statut de centre du monde pour l'amener dans le bois, c'est-à-dire à la périphérie du domaine de sa mère, situation marginale dans laquelle *lui* trouve son centre. C'est ce qui explique le changement de focalisation dans les trois dernières pages de la nouvelle. L'« enfant » est décrite de l'extérieur car elle ne contrôle plus le récit. En fait, le narrateur oscille entre une position de surplomb et un point de vue qui suit encore partiellement le regard de la fillette, mais qui nous installe également dans la vision floue de Powell (derrière ses lunettes parsemées de gouttes d'eau), nous donnant à voir de l'intérieur sa nostalgie rageuse pour ce monde pastoral qu'il préfère détruire faute de pouvoir vraiment le posséder. Ou plutôt, on pourrait dire que la narration superpose deux regards, nous montrant la jeune fille soudain capable d'imaginer ce que voit le garçon. L'expérience du décentrement, en changeant son angle de vue, a modifié durablement sa perception du monde.

L'intrus

Cette mise en forme spatiale de la diégèse se retrouve dans plusieurs autres nouvelles. L'arrivée d'un intrus qui vient briser l'équilibre d'un univers bien ordonné est le moteur de l'intrigue de « A Stroke of Good Fortune » (l'enfant dont on ne veut pas), « A Good Man Is Hard to Find » (le « Désaxé »), « The Life You Save May Be Your Own » (le vagabond, Mr. Shiftlet), « The Displaced Person » (Mr. Guizac, l'étranger dont on ne comprend ni la langue ni les codes de comportement), « A Temple of the Holy Ghost » (les visiteuses du week-end, leurs compagnons et l'hermaphrodite), « Good Country People » (le vendeur de bibles), « Greenleaf » (le taureau des frères Greenleaf), « A View of the Woods » (la machine), « The Comforts of Home » (Star Drake, la nymphomane), « Everything That Rises Must Converge » (les Noirs dans le bus récemment déségrégué), « The Lame Shall Enter First » (le garçon des rues au pied bot), « Judgement Day » ainsi que « The Geranium » (les Noirs des villes).

La liste ci-dessus permet de dégager les constantes du microcosme o'connorien. L'univers bien ordonné correspond généralement au monde des possédants (propriétaires de fermes et de terres prospères) comme le clame Mrs. Turpin dans « Revelation ». Les intrus se rangent globalement dans trois catégories : les pauvres Blancs (souvent affligés d'infirmités comme le manchot, Mr. Shiftlet ou le boiteux, Rufus Johnson) – surtout lorsqu'ils menacent de renverser l'ordre social (Powell, Rufus) ou la hiérarchie économique (les frères

Greenleaf) ; les Noirs et les étrangers – en particulier lorsqu'ils ne sont pas à leur place (sociale ou géographique) et les fondamentalistes protestants (le pasteur de « The River », les adeptes de la « Church of God » dans « A Temple of the Holy Ghost », le vendeur de bibles dans « Good Country People »). Comme on le voit, ces individus ne sont menaçants que lorsqu'ils sont « déplacés », c'est-à-dire lorsqu'ils sortent de leur environnement habituel ou autorisé ou lorsqu'ils prétendent changer de position sociale.

Cette confrontation entre groupes antagonistes rend compte de la réalité socio-économique des années 1950 au cours desquelles la plupart des nouvelles d'O'Connor ont été écrites. La période de prospérité de l'après Deuxième Guerre mondiale a contribué à la déstructuration du tissu social en permettant la montée des classes moyennes, voire populaires. C'est ce qui perturbe le plus Mrs. May, la protagoniste de « Greenleaf ». D'autant plus que, pour la plupart des possédants sudistes, cette déstructuration vient rappeler (quand ce n'est pas renforcer) la perte de statut social et de pouvoir économique des propriétaires de plantations après la guerre de Sécession. Par ailleurs, les années 1950 sont également marquées par d'intenses mouvements de contestation de la part des Noirs qui demandent la fin du régime de ségrégation. En 1955, ils boycottent les autobus ségrégués de Montgomery, Alabama pendant 381 jours et obtiennent qu'une décision de la Cour Suprême mette fin à cette situation inégalitaire. C'est l'événement qui est en filigrane derrière la nouvelle « Everything that Rises Must Converge ». Enfin, sur le plan religieux, la famille O'Connor, d'origine irlandaise, appartient à la minorité catholique qui est plus ou moins bien acceptée dans le Sud massivement protestant. En fait, avant d'habiter à Milledgeville, Flannery O'Connor avait passé les treize premières années de sa vie à Savannah, ville connue pour sa tolérance qui, en 1794, avait accueilli les réfugiés catholiques blancs fuyant l'insurrection de Toussaint l'Ouverture à Haïti, et cela bien que l'État de Géorgie dans son ensemble ait voté une charte interdisant la pratique du catholicisme sur son territoire. On voit donc que le sentiment de vivre dans une enclave protégée pouvait correspondre à l'expérience personnelle de l'auteur et que l'obsession de ses personnages pour les barrières et les lignes de démarcation de toutes sortes renvoyait en grande partie à une réalité typiquement sudiste.

Dans le petit théâtre o'connorien, les grands drames de l'Histoire sont cependant rarement mentionnés directement mais déplacés et reconfigurés dans un espace restreint où chaque personnage joue un rôle à la fois intensément personnel et profondément emblématique. Le sens de la menace, qui plane sur les années qui suivent le conflit mondial et sur la période de la Guerre Froide, se retrouve dans le sentiment d'insécurité des protagonistes de ses nouvelles. Et là encore, comme on peut le voir dans « The Displaced Person », c'est par le biais de la représentation et de l'utilisation de l'espace que le drame se joue. Mr. Guizac, ce rescapé que l'internement dans des camps n'était pas parvenu à exterminer, va périr aux États-Unis avec la complicité conjuguée des pauvres Blancs, des Noirs et des petits propriétaires terriens. Tous vont finalement se liguer pour éliminer cet élément exogène qui perturbe l'équilibre et la stabilité des lieux. Même si certains d'entre eux pouvaient trouver leur compte dans la présence du « réfugié » (la propriétaire à qui il faisait gagner de l'argent et le Noir à qui il promettait le mariage avec une jolie jeune fille de sa famille), tous préfèrent « le Diable qu'ils connaissent », c'est-à-dire l'organisation bien rodée d'une structure de pouvoir où chacun sait quelle est sa place et quelles sont ses limites, où chaque catégorie d'individus est complémentaire des autres et où tout le monde est interdépendant. La peur de l'inconnu est plus forte que les avantages dus au changement.

Cette problématique est mise en place dès l'ouverture présentée en focalisation interne sur la conscience de l'employée, Mrs. Shortley. Celle-ci s'est installée en position dominante sur une petite colline près de la maison d'où elle peut surveiller l'arrivée de la famille de réfugiés polonais. De son poste d'observation elle a la même vue que la fillette de « A Circle in the Fire » ou des deux Lucynell Crater, mère et fille, dans « The Life You Save May Be Your Own », une vue qui part des confins de la propriété délimitée cette fois par l'horizon sur lequel se dessine « a ragged *wall* of cloud » (194, c'est moi qui souligne) et s'arrête aux marches de la maison où la propriétaire, Mrs. McIntyre, s'apprête à recevoir les étrangers comme des invités de marque. Elle peut ainsi suivre la progression de la voiture depuis le moment où celle-ci s'engage « down the red clay road that turned off from the highway » (194) et pénètre à l'intérieur du cercle protégé de la ferme, pénétration dont le caractère menaçant est souligné d'emblée :

> Her arms were folded and as she mounted the prominence, she might have been the giant wife of the countryside, come out *at some sign of danger to see what the trouble was.* (194, c'est moi qui souligne)

Le soleil qui apparaît derrière les nuages, véritable corrélat objectif de l'arrivée des réfugiés, est d'ailleurs décrit comme un « intruder ». Les bras croisés sur la poitrine de Mrs. Shortley trahissent son repliement sur elle-même et son besoin de sécurité. Plus tard, lorsque Mrs McIntyre voudra congédier le Polonais, elle adoptera la même position défensive, les bras repliés comme pour former un bouclier :

> When he had passed her and rounded the turn, she *climbed to the top of the slope* and stood *with her arms folded* and looked out grimly over the field. [...]
> She narrowed her gaze until it *closed entirely around the diminishing* figure on the tractor as if she were *watching him through a gunsight.* [...] and she stood there, a small black-hatted, black-smocked figure with an aging cherubic face, and *folded arms* as if she were equal to anything. But her heart was beating as if some interior violence had already been done to her. She opened her eyes *to include the whole field* so that *the figure on the tractor was no larger than a grasshopper in her widened view.* (224, c'est moi qui souligne)

On notera qu'à ce moment décisif, Mrs. McIntyre éprouve également le besoin de se positionner sur une petite colline pour avoir une vue d'ensemble de sa propriété et surtout pour pouvoir réduire la taille de l'étranger à celle d'un insecte dont il paraîtra plus simple de se débarrasser. Car ce qui avait dérangé Mrs Shortley le jour de l'arrivée de la famille polonaise, c'était précisément le fait que : « they looked like other people » (195) et qu'il semblait donc difficile de les mettre dans une catégorie à part et de les exclure d'emblée.

Par un effet de renversement, ce qui rend les étrangers menaçants ici n'est pas tant qu'ils représentent le Mal (bien que les Shortley, par glissement sémantique, n'hésiteront pas à les assimiler à leurs bourreaux européens), mais qu'au contraire, en étant exactement ce que Mrs. McIntyre souhaitait, c'est-à-dire honnêtes et travailleurs, ils la concurrencent sur son propre terrain. Elle ira même jusqu'à rêver qu'ils s'approprient ses terres et s'installent dans sa maison. Du coup, les Noirs voleurs et les pauvres Blancs paresseux ne lui apparaissent plus comme des fléaux : leur infériorité déclarée et acceptée par tous devient indispensable à la reconnaissance de sa supériorité.

Le territoire qu'il lui faut défendre contre ces envahisseurs potentiels est symbolisé par deux lieux associés à leur propriétaire initial, le Juge, premier mari de Mrs McIntyre : d'une part le bureau du vieil homme gardé intact au cœur de la maison et d'autre part sa tombe au milieu d'un champ de blé. Le visage du Juge, décrit comme « a clay pink pitted and tracked with mysterious prehistoric-looking marks as if he had been unearthed among fossils » (218), l'identifie étroitement à la terre à laquelle il semble appartenir (plutôt qu'il ne la possède) depuis des temps immémoriaux. Son aspect de « fossile préhistorique » traduit le désir de permanence et de durée d'un système qu'il aurait voulu pérenne. Malgré cela, le Juge n'a jamais pu sauver la ferme de ses créanciers et a laissé à sa femme un bien hypothéqué qu'elle a conservé tant bien que mal sans pouvoir l'empêcher de perdre de sa valeur. La déchéance progressive du lieu est marquée par la diminution du nombre de travailleurs noirs (survivance de l'esclavage) et de paons (symboles de luxe, d'oisiveté et de beauté) et par les tares et les vices des deux autres maris successifs de Mrs McIntyre : la folie et l'alcoolisme.

Le bureau du vieil homme, au centre de la maison, est dépeint comme une « chapelle » et contient lui-même : « a small safe, empty but locked, set like a tabernacle in the center of it » (221). Quant à la tombe, elle était autrefois ornée d'un angelot choisi par le Juge pour sa ressemblance avec son épouse. Au moment du récit, le coffre-fort est vide et la tombe a été dépouillée de son ange gardien par d'anciens métayers. Le centre autour duquel gravite l'existence de Mrs McIntyre, et qu'elle vénère par-dessus tout, n'est plus qu'une coquille vide, dénuée de sens. La touche finale apportée à cette désappropriation/désacralisation graduelle des lieux est symboliquement représentée par les cercles concentriques décrits par la « faucheuse » de Mr. Guizac qui enserre la tombe du Juge et, telle la Parque, semble vouloir faire disparaître définitivement le monde que ce dernier avait connu et dont, cyniquement, il avait déjà prévu la fin :

> The road ran through a shadowy pine thicket and ended *on top of a hill that rolled fan-wise* down and up again in a broad expanse of tassled green. Mr. Guizac was cutting from the outside of the field *in a circular path to the center* where the graveyard was all but hidden by the corn (221-222) […]
> By nightfall, the Displaced Person would have worked his way *around and around* until there would be *nothing on either side of the hills* but the stubble, and *down in the center*, risen *like an island*, the graveyard where the Judge lay grinning *under his desecrated monument*. (224, c'est moi qui souligne)

Si, comme on le voit dans cette scène, Mr. Guizac trace un motif circulaire qui va de la périphérie vers le centre, Mrs. McIntyre en revanche sera amenée à effectuer le mouvement inverse. Pour annoncer à son employé qu'elle a décidé de le renvoyer, elle sera forcée de quitter le cocon de sa maison pour venir le rejoindre aux confins de la propriété, dans le hangar dont il occupe le centre :

> The countryside seemed to be receding from *the little circle of noise around the shed.* Mr. Guizac was squatting on the ground beside the small tractor (233, c'est moi qui souligne)

Le meurtre du Polonais, dont elle se fait la complice, scelle sa dépossession des lieux, car la scène, à jamais figée (« frozen ») dans sa mémoire, la rend étrangère à elle-même et à son environnement :

> She only stared at him for she was too shocked by her experience to be quite herself. Her mind was not taking hold of all that was happening. She felt she was in some foreign country where the people bent over the body were natives, and she watched like a stranger while the dead man was carried away in the ambulance. (235)

Mr. Guizac est devenu « the dead man ». Il n'est plus « the Displaced Person », car sa mort rend impossible son retour où que ce soit. Son ultime demeure aura été cette ferme et, d'une certaine façon, il prend ainsi la place du Juge qui, jusque-là, était la dernière personne à avoir trouvé la mort en ces lieux. Comme lui, dans cet endroit, « he [will] always [be] at home » (218).

Le corps-sanctuaire

Les changements importants dans la vie des protagonistes surviennent donc lorsqu'ils sortent de leur orbite habituelle pour se placer dans celle d'un autre personnage. C'est ce qui se produit pour la jeune Joy/Hulga dans « Good Country People » au moment où elle abandonne toutes ses défenses et où elle accepte de devenir dépendante du vendeur de bibles en lui révélant son secret le plus intime (« it was like surrendering to him completely. It was like losing her own life and finding it again, miraculously, in his », 289). Et peu importe que le garçon n'ait pas été le modèle d'innocence qu'elle imaginait. Ce que l'expérience lui apporte, c'est la possibilité de sortir de soi ou encore, comme elle exhortait sa mère à le faire, de découvrir l'Autre en soi (« Woman ! do you ever look inside ? Do you ever look inside and see what you are *not* ? », 276). Or, ce changement de regard sur elle-même ne peut se produire qu'une fois qu'elle s'est laissée dépouiller des accessoires « sacrés » qui lui tiennent lieu de personnalité : ses lunettes d'intellectuelle et la jambe de bois qui signe sa « différence » d'avec le reste du monde. Et, bien sûr, cette épiphanie n'est envisageable que dans un espace excentré : le grenier d'une grange située à l'extrême limite de la propriété.

Pour les personnages de Flannerv O'Connor, la maison (« home ») est le refuge par excellence. Et nous avons vu avec « A Circle in the Fire » qu'elle pouvait même devenir une extension du protagoniste, à la fois projection extériorisée de son ego et seconde peau protectrice. Lorsque cette maison est à son tour menacée d'intrusion, il reste encore à ses occupants la possibilité de se replier sur une pièce privilégiée, comme le fait Thomas dans « The Comforts of Home ». Cette « chambre intérieure » (formule que j'emprunte à Carson McCullers dans *The Heart is a Lonely Hunter*) est à la fois un espace littéral, décrit à l'aide de détails réalistes, et un espace figuré renvoyant au moi intime du personnage, à son intériorité, à ses pensées. De sorte que toute tentative de pénétration dans ces lieux, si elle peut toujours se lire, à un certain niveau, comme une agression sexuelle, équivaut également à un viol de la conscience. Lorsque la mère de Thomas introduit une jeune nymphomane dans la maison qu'elle partage avec son fils, celui-ci redoute moins les avances sexuelles de la jeune fille que la « souillure » de son espace secret représentée par la présence quotidienne de cette étrangère dans son univers familier :

> Thomas kept to his room or the den. His home was to him home, workshop, church, as personal as the shell of a turtle and as necessary. (395) […]
> He cared nothing about the gun, but the thought of Sarah Ham's hands sliding among his papers infuriated him. Now even his study was contaminated. The only place left untouched by her was his bedroom.
> That night she entered it. (398).

Asbury, l'écrivain raté de « The Enduring Chill », trouve aussi refuge dans la chambre de malade qu'il occupe au cœur de la maison de sa mère. Mais au-delà de la chambre, pour ce jeune homme qui se considère comme un intellectuel sophistiqué (à l'instar de Joy/Hulga dans « Good Country People »), c'est d'abord le corps souffrant qu'il convient de valoriser, car il est le symbole d'une conscience torturée. Et plus ce corps présente de handicaps, plus il prend d'importance à ses yeux. Bien qu'Asbury se voit en rêve mort et enterré dans le caveau familial, il préfère en fait cultiver son image de moribond, car il ne peut se résoudre à perdre définitivement son esprit supérieur. Le corps, la chambre et les limites de la propriété se superposent pour représenter l'enveloppe matérielle qui devrait sauvegarder ses facultés intellectuelles contre toute agression extérieure :

> He shuddered and turned his head quickly the other way and stared out the window. A blinding red-gold sun moved serenely from under a purple cloud. Below it the treeline was black against a crimson sky. It formed a brittle wall, standing as if it were the frail defense he had set up in his mind to protect him from what was to come. (382)

Mais pour cet athée convaincu, la difficulté consiste à définir la nature même de cet esprit qu'il cherche à défendre. Parfois il se le représente comme pure matière, réduit au sang qui coule dans ses veines et que le médecin veut analyser cherchant ainsi à percer à jour son moi intime :

> He pushed Asbury's sleeve up and tied the tube around his upper arm. Then he took out a syringe and prepared to find the vein, humming a hymn as he pressed the needle in. Asbury lay with a rigid outraged stare while the privacy of his blood was invaded by this idiot. (367)

À d'autres moments, il est conscient que, dans son monde sans transcendance, cet « esprit » ne saurait être qu'un potentiel, une faculté de penser ou de créer qu'il aurait pu (mais n'a pas su) remplir par des œuvres d'art. Il en est alors réduit à s'accrocher à la matérialité du monde qui l'entoure et qui forme la seule réalité de son existence absurde et désespérée :

> He felt as if he were a shell that had to be filled with something but he did not know what. He began to take note of everything in the room as if for the last time – the ridiculous antique furniture, the pattern in the rug, the silly picture his mother had replaced. (378)

Pour l'écrivain catholique, le corps d'Asbury n'est qu'un « tabernacle vide » comme le coffre sur le bureau du Juge dans « The Displaced Person » et seul le Saint-Esprit saurait le remplir de manière satisfaisante.

Dans la nouvelle « A Temple of the Holy Ghost », le corps est également l'ultime sanctuaire qui protège l'esprit saint, surtout lorsque ce corps se trouve déplacé, hors des limites de la maison ou du couvent, dans une automobile qui évoque « the last circle of hell » (239). De manière générale, chez Flannery O'Connor, les automobiles, comme la plupart des machines, symbolisent une modernité destructrice. Ce sont des lieux dangereux où l'esprit risque de s'égarer sur des sentiers de perdition, comme l'illustre littéralement la nouvelle « A Good Man Is Hard to Find ». Sarah Ruth, dans « Parker's Back » associe également ce mode de locomotion au péché :

> One of the things she didn't approve of was automobiles. In addition to her other bad qualities, she was forever sniffing up sin. (510)

Seul Mr. Shiftlet de « The Life You Save May Be Your Own » utilise une symbolique positive de la voiture (associée à l'esprit), mais dans l'unique but de tromper la fermière sur ses intentions :

> "Lady, a man is divided into two parts, body and spirit." [...] "The body, lady, is like a house: it don't go anywhere; but the spirit, lady, is like a automobile: always on the move, always..." (152)

Ce qui cause la perte de la jeune Lucynell Crater est son départ dans cette automobile loin du cercle protégé de sa maison. Traduit dans la symbolique de Mr. Shiftlet, cela signifie la dissociation du corps et de l'esprit. Or, pour Flannery O'Connor, adepte de la pensée de Teilhard de Chardin, cette dissociation ne peut en aucun cas conduire au salut. En effet, pour le Jésuite français, qui essaie de concilier science et métaphysique, le monde ne se compose pas de matière d'une part et d'esprit d'autre part, mais d'entités uniques combinant les deux éléments et auxquelles il donne le nom d'Esprit-Matière. D'après lui, la plupart des individus ne perçoivent le monde que par le biais de leurs organes sensoriels et n'en connaissent donc que la face matérielle. Mais pour peu qu'ils se donnent la peine de l'aborder grâce à leur vision intérieure, ils en découvrent alors la dimension spirituelle. C'est pourquoi, dans les nouvelles de Flannery O'Connor, seuls les êtres dotés de double vue ont une chance d'être sauvés. Ceux qui ont été aveuglés toute leur vie ou ne sont capables que d'une perception purement matérielle (et donc partielle) des choses reçoivent parfois *in extremis*, grâce à un choc violent, une révélation de l'autre face du monde, mais, durant l'essentiel du récit, ils évoluent dans un univers désespérément divisé.

9

La maison divisée

Si la division qui hante l'univers de Flannery O'Connor renvoie à la théologie de Teilhard de Chardin, on la retrouve par ailleurs de manière récurrente dans toute la littérature sudiste. Et là encore, il est possible de faire remonter cette tradition à l'un des contes de Poe les plus célèbres : « The Fall of the House of Usher ». Dans ce récit gothique par excellence, la maison des Usher, vieille famille aristocratique, est très étroitement associée à ses occupants. Lorsque le conte débute, elle est dans le même état de délabrement que les derniers descendants de la lignée : Roderick et sa sœur jumelle, Lady Madeline of Usher. La maladie des deux propriétaires des lieux est décrite comme partiellement fantasmatique ou due aux miasmes mortifères qui émanent des douves du château. Ces douves donnent d'ailleurs de la maison une image inversée qui redouble son aspect sinistre, tout comme la maladie de Lady Madeline semble renforcer celle de son frère. Le texte lui-même fonctionne sur une thématique du double puisqu'il comporte plusieurs histoires enchâssées dont les péripéties (l'histoire d'un pèlerin qui demande asile dans une maison où il est amené à tuer un dragon) font écho, en les amplifiant, aux événements du récit-cadre. Mais la fonction de ces effets-miroirs est surtout d'insister sur la construction imaginaire des personnages, sur la façon dont ils rêvent leur vie et sur l'emprise de l'esprit sur le corps et sur la matière. En effet, dès l'instant où Lady Madeline, après avoir été enterrée vivante, sort de sa tombe et vient mourir définitivement dans les bras de son frère, celui-ci ne peut ni ne veut lui survivre et s'écroule à son tour. À ce moment-là, la maison, dont la façade était striée d'une lézarde sur toute la hauteur, se divise et disparaît elle aussi, absorbée avec son image dans les douves qui l'encerclaient.

Comme nous l'avons dit au chapitre précédent, la maison, chez O'Connor, est conçue comme une forteresse destinée à abriter d'abord le corps, puis l'esprit, et elle est menacée de dissolution lorsque la volonté, le désir, l'imaginaire de ses occupants n'est plus là pour la soutenir (voir la fin de « The Displaced Person »). Si la maison ne sombre pas dans des douves, en revanche des lacs réels, artificiels ou fantasmatiques peuvent engloutir les personnages privés de leurs repères, comme Mr. Fortune dans « A View of the Woods » qui s'imagine noyé dans celui qu'il a permis de creuser. Dans « Good Country People », la jeune fille, dépouillée de ses lunettes, a l'impression de voir, dans les prairies environnantes, deux lacs verts dont les eaux enflent et menacent de la faire disparaître :

> She looked away from him off into the hollow sky and then down at a black ridge and then down farther into what appeared to be two green swelling lakes. (287)

Et, bien sûr, il y a la rivière dans laquelle le jeune garçon de « The River » a décidé de se laisser entraîner pour poursuivre son rêve d'un monde meilleur.

Mais ce qui rapproche le plus les nouvelles de Flannery O'Connor du conte de Poe, c'est l'usage de la thématique du double et de la division.

Les personnages et leurs doubles

Comme les jumeaux du conte – différents (de sexe opposé) mais complémentaires et indissociables – les personnages de Flannery O'Connor ont presque tous des doubles indispensables à leur survie en ce monde.

Il y a tout d'abord les « couples » de fermières, propriétaires et employées, que l'on retrouve dans plusieurs nouvelles avec quelques variantes : Mrs. Cope et Mrs. Pritchard de « A Circle in the Fire », Mrs. McIntyre et Mrs. Shortley de « The Displaced Person », Mrs. Hopewell et Mrs. Freeman de « Good Country People » et Mrs. May et Mrs. Greenleaf de « Greenleaf ». Physiquement dissemblables (les employées sont généralement grosses, bavardes et plutôt vulgaires et les propriétaires petites, autoritaires et économes de leurs paroles et de leur argent), elles ont cependant besoin l'une de l'autre et (à l'exception de Mrs. May et Mrs. Greenleaf) passent le plus clair de leur temps ensemble dans la cuisine de la grande maison. Mrs. Freeman, par exemple, arrive tous les jours aux heures des repas pour parler de ses filles, un coude appuyé sur le réfrigérateur. Mrs. McIntyre, qui a décidé de ne pas lutter contre la curiosité exacerbée de Mrs. Shortley, lui a donné des responsabilités et sillonne avec elle la propriété pour surveiller le travail de ses métayers. Contrairement à son ancien employeur, elle s'accommode très bien du caractère envahissant de Mrs Shortley et se trouve très affectée par le départ, puis la mort, de cette dernière :

> She realized all at once that it was Mrs. Shortley she had been missing. She had had no one to talk to since Mrs. Shortley left, and she ran to the door, expecting to see her heaving herself up the steps. (226-227) […]
> It took Mrs. McIntyre three days to get over Mrs. Shortley's death. She told herself that anyone would have thought they were kin. She rehired Mr. Shortley to do farm work though actually she didn't want him without his wife. (227)

Nous avons vu que, dans la structure hiérarchisée de l'exploitation agricole, chacune jouait son rôle et remplissait une fonction nécessaire à l'équilibre de cette microsociété. Pourtant, Mrs. McIntyre et Mrs. Shortley pourraient avoir l'air d'être parentes (« kin »). Et peu de choses, de fait, les différencient si ce n'est la conscience d'appartenir à des classes différentes : elles sont aussi ignorantes l'une que l'autre, elles cultivent les mêmes préjugés (racistes, en particulier) et elles débitent les mêmes clichés. Mais c'est bien précisément parce que l'écart entre elles est si ténu qu'il est indispensable à la plus privilégiée des deux de le maintenir. Or, les gens de leur entourage (et surtout leurs enfants) s'ingénient à brouiller les pistes en s'adonnant à des jeux de permutations de rôles.

Ainsi, dans « Greenleaf », les fils de Mrs. May, Scofield et Wesley, qui ont reçu une bonne éducation mais n'ont pas aussi bien réussi dans la vie qu'elle l'espérait, s'acharnent à désespérer leur mère en parlant le dialecte nasal des frères Greenleaf, les jumeaux O.T et E.T. Parfois Scofield va même jusqu'à prétendre qu'à la mort de sa mère il épousera quelqu'un comme Mrs. Greenleaf. Or cette perspective correspond aux pires craintes de Mrs. May, celle de voir les fils Greenleaf s'élever dans la société et occuper la position qui, d'après elle, devrait revenir à ses propres enfants, tandis que ces derniers s'enfonceraient inexorablement dans la déchéance. Cet échange de rôles est pourtant déjà en train de s'accomplir : depuis que les jumeaux sont revenus de la guerre couverts de médailles, ils ont pu installer une ferme moderne et prospère grâce à leur pension d'anciens combattants et vivent confortablement. Les inquiétudes de

Mrs. May sont métaphorisées par l'intrusion dans sa ferme d'un taureau sans pedigree appartenant à O.T et E.T. qui menace d'inséminer ses vaches laitières et donc de dévaloriser son troupeau. Et la perte de puissance de la propriétaire des lieux est, ici encore, figurée par des images de cercles dont les centres changent de valeur au cours du récit. En effet, si au début Mr. Greenleaf manifeste son respect craintif de Mrs. May en ne l'abordant jamais directement (« He walked on the perimeter of some invisible circle and if you wanted to look him in the face, you had to move and get in front of him », 313) et donc en la plaçant au centre d'une structure de pouvoir, à la fin, refusant d'exécuter ses ordres, il la laisse seule au milieu d'une prairie en forme d'« arène » où le taureau peut aisément la prendre pour cible (like a bull's eye) et l'immoler sous ses yeux tandis qu'il est en train d'approcher « on the outside of some invisible circle » (334), c'est-à-dire (délibérément ?) trop tard.

O.T. et E.T. se ressemblent traits pour traits et les frères May sont décrits comme leurs doubles inversés : « an ugly family resemblance showed between them » (327). Si les jumeaux sont des garçons agréables qui ne se disputent jamais, les deux autres se haïssent et vont jusqu'à se battre dans la cuisine familiale. Cette image en miroir souligne l'inversion des valeurs sur lesquelles repose la nouvelle – inversion dont Mrs. May prend conscience avec déchirement :

> "O.T and E.T. are fine boys," she said. "They ought to have been my sons." The thought of this was so horrible that her vision of Wesley was blurred at once by a wall of tears. All she saw was his dark shape, rising quickly from the table. "And you two," she cried, "you two should have belonged to that woman!" (321)

La permutation des rôles et des valeurs est aussi le schéma sur lequel fonctionne « Everything that Rises Must Converge ». Dans ce récit, Julian, le fils de Mrs. Chestny, veut donner une leçon à sa mère pour la convaincre définitivement de la perte de son statut social dominant. Pour ce faire, il choisit, de préférence à une longue démonstration verbale, un déplacement spatial qui dessine de manière concrète les nouvelles configurations d'une société devenue multiraciale et, officiellement du moins, égalitaire. Dans l'autobus récemment déségrégué qui les conduit au YWCA (centre d'activités culturelles et sportives destiné, en principe, aux couches défavorisées de la population), Julian choisit de s'asseoir à côté d'un Noir, ce que sa mère bien sûr désapprouve :

> The woman with the red and white canvas sandals had risen at the same time the Negro sat down and had gone further back in the bus and taken the seat of the woman who had got off. His mother leaned forward and cast her an approving look.
> Julian rose, *crossed the aisle*, and sat down in the place of the woman with the canvas sandals. *From this position*, he looked serenely *across* at his mother. Her face had turned an angry red. He stared at her, making his eyes *the eyes of a stranger*. He felt his tension suddenly as if *he had openly declared war on her*. (412, c'est moi qui souligne)

La répétition des termes qui suggèrent le passage d'une position à une autre, la traversée d'une ligne de démarcation (« crossed the aisle », « looked across », « from his position ») évoque une guerre de tranchée, ce qui sera repris explicitement dans le paragraphe suivant par la description du Noir « *entrenched* behind his paper ». Un siècle après la guerre de Sécession, les passagers de l'autobus semblent prêts à en rejouer une version édulcorée sur ce substitut de champ de bataille. Et la comparaison ne s'avère pas si anodine, puisque l'épisode se termine par une mort : celle de la descendante d'un ancien gouverneur de l'Etat dont la nostalgie pour l'époque des plantations est restée intacte jusqu'à la fin. La défaite est donc consommée, mais la nostalgie ne disparaîtra pas pour autant puisqu'au fond, Julian, le donneur de leçon, a toujours cultivé une attitude ambiguë par rapport à la perte de position sociale de ses ancêtres, symbolisée par la grande maison en ruine :

> He never spoke of [the decayed mansion] without contempt or thought of it without longing. He had seen it once when he was a child before it had been sold. The double stairways had rotted and been torn down. Negroes were living in it. But it remained in his mind as his mother had known it. It appeared in his dreams regularly. He would stand on the wide porch, listening to the rustle of oak leaves, then wander through the high-ceilinged hall into the parlor that opened onto it and gaze at the worn rugs and faded draperies. It occurred to him that it was he, not she, who would have appreciated it. He preferred its threadbare elegance to anything he could name and it was because of it that the neighborhoods they had lived in had been a torment to him. (408-409)

Cette nostalgie du passé, Julian s'efforce pourtant de la refouler, plus peut-être pour régler des comptes avec sa mère que par conviction profonde. Ou encore parce qu'il se sent obligé d'adopter les vues radicales des gens qu'il a fréquentés à l'université et qui servent surtout, là encore, à le conforter dans son sentiment de supériorité vis-à-vis de sa mère. Car la satire d'O'Connor s'exerce aussi bien à l'encontre des petits-bourgeois autosatisfaits que des intellectuels prétentieux. Les uns et les autres sont présentés comme les deux faces d'une même réalité limitée. Chacun renvoie à l'autre une image de son aveuglement, mais aucun n'est lucide sur lui-même. Cette structure en miroir, ou en chassé-croisé, est soulignée dans la scène où Julian se trouve assis à côté d'une grosse femme noire dont le fils est installé en face, à côté de sa propre mère :

> Meanwhile the woman was bearing down upon the empty seat beside Julian. *To his annoyance*, she squeezed herself into it. He saw his mother's face change as the woman settled herself next to him and he realized with satisfaction that this was more objectionable to her than it was to him. Her face seemed almost gray and there was a look of dull recognition in her eyes, as if suddenly she had sickened at some awful confrontation. *Julian saw that it was because she and the woman had, in a sense, swapped sons.* Though his mother would not realize the symbolic significance of this, she would feel it. His amusement showed plainly on his face. (415, c'est moi qui souligne)

En fait, Julian n'est pas particulièrement enchanté de la présence de la femme noire à ses côtés (« to his annoyance... »). Sa satisfaction ne découle que de la possibilité de profiter de la situation pour défendre une position de principe : montrer à sa mère qu'il pourrait échanger sa place dans le monde avec celle du garçon noir, ce qu'il ne souhaite pas véritablement. Le passage montre par ailleurs que sa prétendue lucidité est mise en défaut. Alors qu'il croit avoir décelé un symbole dans l'échange des enfants (« Julian *saw* that it was *because*... »), il n'a tout simplement pas perçu que le changement d'expression de sa mère était dû à la découverte d'un chapeau identique au sien sur la tête de la voisine de Julian. Outre son solipsisme, le jeune homme trahit son profond narcissisme : il ne s'intéresse qu'à ce qui va modifier sa propre relation à sa mère. Il souhaiterait que cette dernière soit totalement absorbée par lui car il voudrait pouvoir contrôler à chaque instant l'effet produit sur elle par ses moindres faits et gestes. Alors qu'il entend fustiger le sentiment de supériorité sociale de sa mère, il ne parvient qu'à révéler son propre désir de domination.

Lorsqu'il comprend enfin la situation (sa mère et la femme noire portent le même chapeau), il voit également le parti qu'il va pouvoir en tirer pour marquer des points dans cette bataille purement personnelle. Pourtant, là encore, il est convaincu d'agir avec une parfaite objectivité :

> For a moment he had an uncomfortable sense of her innocence, but it lasted only a second before *principle rescued him. Justice entitled him to laugh.* His grin hardened until it said to her as plainly as if he were saying aloud :

> Your punishment exactly fits your pettiness. *This should teach you a permanent lesson.* (416, c'est moi qui souligne)

Par cette dernière phrase, l'écrivain catholique suggère que Julian est coupable du péché d'orgueil absolu. En prétendant infliger une leçon *permanente* à sa mère, il se place dans la position du Dieu du Jugement Dernier. Et lorsqu'il veut pousser plus loin la leçon en martelant : « That was the whole colored race which will no longer take your condescending pennies. *That was your black double* » (419, c'est moi qui souligne), il énonce certes une vérité, mais il ne voit pas le miroir qui lui est tendu à son tour, miroir dans lequel il pourrait reconnaître sa propre attitude condescendante, lui qui est incapable de compassion. Ainsi, au bout du compte, Flannery O'Connor renverse-t-elle l'équilibre des forces entre les deux personnages, puisque Julian finira par apprendre à ses dépens la leçon que sa mère, elle aussi, avait essayé de lui inculquer – celle de la prééminence du « cœur » sur l'intellect :

> He thrust his face toward her and hissed, "True culture is in the mind, the *mind*," he said, and tapped his head, "the mind."
> "It's in the heart," she said (409-410)

L'autobus, espace neutre et intermédiaire entre la maison (« Home ») et le point de destination (« the Y / why ? ») est finalement devenu un lieu de communion où Julian a fait l'apprentissage de l'Autre. Non pas de l'Autre étranger et lointain, mais du proche et du familier dont le mystère n'est pas moins impénétrable. Arrivant tout illuminé en haut de la colline, l'autobus où l'on est assis de part et d'autre d'une allée comme à l'église et où l'on doit déposer un « token » (une hostie ?) pour faire partie du groupe, a été pour lui le lieu d'une ultime révélation.

En dehors des fermières et de leurs employées, les autres « couples » qui fonctionnent comme des doubles dans les nouvelles de Flannery O'Connor sont souvent composés de parents et d'enfants ou parfois d'un grand-père avec son petit-fils ou sa petite-fille. Les récits qui mettent en scène des relations mère/fils sont, nous l'avons vu, « Everything that Rises Must Converge », mais aussi « A Good man Is Hard to Find », « Greenleaf », « The Enduring Chill » et « The Comforts of Home ». Les liens mère /fille se trouvent dans « The Life You Save May Be Your Own », « A Circle in the Fire », « A Temple of the Holy Ghost », « Good Country People » et « Revelation ». Les pères et les filles occupent la place centrale de « The Geranium »,

« A Late Encounter with the Enemy » et « Judgement Day ». On ne trouve de « couple » père/fils que dans « The Lame Shall Enter First », un couple marié dans « Parker's Back », un grand-père et un petit-fils dans « The Artificial Nigger » et un autre grand-père avec sa petite-fille dans « A View of the Woods ».

La plupart des relations parents/enfants se déroulent sur un mode antagoniste. Si les personnages sont complémentaires, c'est parce qu'ils sont interdépendants, mais cette dépendance même nourrit de nombreuses rancœurs. Cependant, comme dans « Everything that Rises Must Converge », l'hubris des enfants ne résiste pas à un choc violent et l'expérience de la dépossession les ramène à la fois au sens du réel, à la reconnaissance de l'existence de l'Autre et à la découverte d'une transcendance. La même épiphanie est souvent offerte aux parents coupables de courte vue, voire d'aveuglement total sur le monde. Les deux extrêmes d'un couple d'éléments opposés se rejoignent donc à la fin, même si cette compréhension finale ne survient parfois que juste avant la mort. C'est souvent un principe intermédiaire qui sert de catalyseur au rapprochement entre deux personnages, comme le « nègre artificiel » pour Nelson et son grand-père ou, plus généralement, un étranger ou un « intrus ». Comme nous l'avons vu, la révélation se produit lorsque les protagonistes sortent de leur routine et se trouvent dans un lieu excentré par rapport à leur univers familier. Outre les bois sombres qui bordent les grandes propriétés, il y a aussi les espaces communautaires comme l'autobus que prennent Julian et sa mère et la salle d'attente du médecin de « Revelation ». Ces lieux de transition offrent l'avantage de présenter un échantillonnage presque complet de la société sudiste. Par ailleurs, l'autobus permet d'introduire un sujet d'actualité (les résistances à l'abolition de la ségrégation) et la salle d'attente du médecin une thématique liée au sujet précédent (la société du Sud perçue comme malade).

Les premiers paragraphes de « Revelation » mettent en place une structuration de l'espace destinée à souligner visuellement les changements entre le Vieux Sud et le Nouveau. Mrs. Turpin, qui très vite s'avèrera être le personnage principal et qui se voit comme appartenant à l'élite d'une société fortement hiérarchisée, est placée d'emblée au centre de la pièce :

> She stood looming *at the head* of the magazine table set *in the center of it*, a living demonstration that the room was inadequate and ridiculous. Her

> little bright black eyes took in the patients as *she sized up* the seating situation. (488, c'est moi qui souligne)

L'emploi du terme « sized up » montre que Mrs. Turpin s'arroge le droit de définir et de classer les gens et les lieux. Sa position dominante au milieu de la salle d'attente, près de la table basse, est cependant indirectement minée par la description de cette dernière :

> The table was cluttered with limp-looking magazines and at one end of it there was a big green glass ash tray full of cigarette butts and cotton wads with blood spots on them. If she had had anything to do with the running of the place, that would have been emptied every so often. (489)

Les signes de désordre et de maladie sont laissés apparents (« cigarette butts and cotton wads with blood spots ») et Mrs. Turpin, dont le désir de contrôle sur son environnement est irrépressible, révèle à la fois son besoin d'ordre (elle voudrait vider les cendriers) et sa volonté de cacher les manifestations trop visibles de la maladie. En cela, elle trahit d'emblée l'aveuglement sur lequel repose sa conception du monde. Car ce monde a bien changé puisque les hommes ne s'y comportent plus en « gentlemen » (le vieux monsieur fait semblant de dormir pour ne pas avoir à lui laisser sa chaise) et les « white trash », qui ne respectent plus les gens de la bonne société, ne savent même pas inculquer un minimum de bonnes manières à leurs enfants (personne ne dit au petit garçon de se pousser pour faire de la place à Mrs. Turpin sur le canapé). Le fait que la riche fermière se sente à l'étroit dans cette nouvelle société moins glorieuse et brillante que celle du « Vieux Sud » est métaphorisé par sa difficulté à s'encastrer dans le siège moderne de la salle d'attente (« Mrs. Turpin eased into the vacant chair, which held her tight as a corset. » I wish I could reduce, « she said, and rolled her eyes and gave a comic sigh », 489). Le « corset » que cette chaise évoque pour elle renvoie à l'attirail de séduction de la Belle du Sud. Mais son désir de « réduire » son poids (ce qui voudrait dire ici s'ajuster à de nouvelles circonstances) est contredit par le mode comique sur lequel elle profère cette affirmation. En cela, elle s'oppose à Mrs. Chestny qui a décidé d'aller à une « reducing class » pour s'adapter, en quelque sorte, aux « reduced circumstances » dans lesquelles se trouve à présent sa classe sociale. D'ailleurs, de manière générale, la plupart des nouvelles de Flannery O'Connor mettent en jeu une dialectique similaire du débordement et de la contrainte. Et les cadres de ses univers bien organisés finissent toujours par voler en éclats. Ici, c'est par la réaction inattendue d'une jeune intellectuelle, qui lance son livre au visage de Mrs. Turpin, que la surface apparemment étale de ce microcosme social sera brisée, exposant au grand jour la vanité de son autosuffisance bien pensante. À la fin cependant Mrs. Turpin réagira au choc de manière surprenante en reconnaissant une sorte de parenté, de compréhension intime entre elle et la jeune fille :

> Mrs. Turpin's head cleared and her power of motion returned. She leaned forward until she was looking directly into the fierce brilliant eyes. There was no doubt in her mind that the girl did know her, knew her in some intense and personal way, beyond time and place and condition. "What you got to say to me ?" she asked hoarsely and held her breath, waiting, as for a revelation. (500)

La « révélation » dont Mrs. Turpin fait l'expérience s'accompagne d'un élargissement de son champ de vision (« The girl fell with a thud and Mrs. Turpin's vision suddenly reversed itself and saw everything large instead of small », 499), mais aussi de la perception des souffrances de la jeune fille clouée au sol par une infirmière pendant que le médecin enfonce la longue aiguille d'une seringue dans son bras. Transposition de la crucifixion, cette scène de torture évoquant la Passion du Christ secoue les certitudes de la fermière qui intuitivement comprend son lien, au regard de Dieu, avec le reste de l'humanité souffrante, comme la grand-mère de « A Good Man Is Hard to Find » avait perçu, contre toute attente, sa parenté avec le « Désaxé ».

Mais cette révélation n'est pas donnée à tout le monde et certains protagonistes des nouvelles font au contraire l'expérience d'une séparation finale qui les rend étrangers à leur entourage et les laisse seuls dans un univers déserté par le souffle de l'Esprit.

L'expérience de la division

Au début de « A View of the Woods », le vieux Mr. Fortune se flatte de la ressemblance qu'il croit déceler entre lui et sa petite-fille, Mary. Le visage de la fillette est d'ailleurs décrit par la voix narrative comme : « a small replica of the old man's » (336). Par la suite, le récit nous installe en focalisation interne dans la conscience du grand-père qui trace un portrait on ne peut plus laudatif de l'enfant. On devine déjà que cette description est essentiellement narcissique et que Mary sert de miroir au vieillard qui peut ainsi s'enorgueillir d'un certain nombre de qualités par personne interposée :

> No one was particularly glad that Mary Fortune looked like her grandfather except the old man himself. He thought it added greatly to her attractiveness. He thought she was the smartest and the prettiest child he had ever seen and he let the rest of them know that if, IF that was, he left anything to anybody, it would be Mary Fortune he left it to. She was now nine, short and broad like himself, with his very light blue eyes, his wide prominent forehead, his steady penetrating scowl and his rich florid complexion; but she was like him on the inside too. She had, to a singular degree, his intelligence, his strong will, and his push and drive. Though there was seventy years' difference in their ages, the spiritual distance between them was slight. She was the only member of the family he had any respect for. (336)

Le style indirect classique (« he thought) auquel se mêlent les traces d'oralité du style indirect libre (« if, IF that was ») confirme que ce qui nous est donné à lire représente bien les pensées du vieil homme. Pourtant, il semble que la voix narrative s'immisce encore à l'intérieur de ce discours. On ne sait pas en effet si c'est vraiment au grand-père qu'il faut attribuer le choix des termes « short and broad », « penetrating scowl » et « florid complexion » qui ne s'accordent guère avec les adjectifs « attractive » et « pretty ». Il semble, en fait, que le mélange des deux voix vise à miner les propos de Mr. Fortune, stratégie d'ailleurs mise en place dès la première phrase qui introduit un doute concernant l'objectivité du vieil homme. Par ailleurs, la répétition de l'adjectif possessif « his » fait de ce tableau un portrait en creux de Mr. Fortune, mais un portrait où dominent les consonnes sifflantes qui suggèrent déjà « le serpent dans le jardin » – image qui sera utilisée plus tard pour décrire Mr. Tilman, l'associé (ou l'âme damnée) du grand-père. Si Mary Fortune est un double de son grand-père, c'est son double angélique et tôt ou tard dans la narration cette différence se devait d'apparaître. Elle se manifeste en effet lorsque la fillette s'oppose à sa décision de vendre le terrain devant la maison, celui qui permet d'avoir « une vue sur la forêt ». L'image que Mary lui renvoie de lui-même est alors totalement négative, mais, à ce stade, le grand-père l'interprète comme un changement surprenant chez la petite fille et non comme une réaction à son propre comportement auquel il ne voit rien à redire :

> There in the little rectangular opening of hair was his face looking back at him, but it was a reflection not of his present expression but of the darker one that indicated his displeasure. (342)

Mr. Fortune avait pourtant déjà eu l'occasion de voir que sa petite-fille pouvait défier toutes ses attentes en prenant la défense de son père qui la bat et que le vieil homme déteste. Sa façon d'exprimer son incompréhension de la situation se manifestait par l'utilisation de renversements de termes dans un jeu d'oppositions destiné à traduire son sens de l'absurde : « "And black is white," the old man piped, "and night is day" » (343). Pourtant le texte montre qu'il est inconsciemment perturbé, sinon influencé, par la façon de voir de la fillette. Lorsqu'elle lui explique ses raisons de vouloir garder la « pelouse » intacte, par trois fois, il répète ses paroles sous forme de questions, les lui renvoyant en écho :

> "We won't be able to see the woods across the road," she said.
> The old man stared at her. "The woods across the road ?" *he repeated.*
> We won't be able to see the view," she said.
> "The view ?" *He repeated.*
> "The woods," she said, "we won't be able to see the woods from the porch."
> "The woods from the porch ?" *he repeated.* (342, c'est moi qui souligne)

Les répétitions sonnent creux et rythment les phrases comme des battements de tambour accompagnant une mélodie en langue étrangère (voir d'ailleurs l'importance des langues étrangères dans d'autres nouvelles, comme « The Displaced Person », pour suggérer le mystère et l'ineffable). Mais le vieillard, figé dans son rationalisme et sa croyance au progrès, n'est pas capable d'attribuer une dimension symbolique au réel. Plus tard, dans sa chambre, il fera une dernière tentative pour comprendre le point de vue de Mary, mais de nouveau sans succès. Sa vision littérale ne dépasse pas la surface des choses : « There was nothing over there to see », 347 ; « A pine trunk is a pine trunk, he said to himself », un peu comme s'il avait dit « A rose is a rose is a rose », mais ne mesurant pas lui-même sur quels abîmes d'interrogations ses remarques apparemment anodines pouvaient ouvrir. Flannery O'Connor donne une clef à ce questionnement : la triple répétition incrédule (trois fois de suite le vieil homme ira regarder les arbres de sa fenêtre) traduit, dans son système de pensée, les trois reniements de Pierre qui refuse d'admettre qu'il connaît le Christ. Le lecteur est libre d'accepter cette symbolique figée ou de la remplacer par un doute plus généralisé qui n'apporte pas le réconfort d'une solution. Certes, la révélation, chez Flannery O'Connor, conduit rarement la sérénité (Asbury découvre « a purifying terror » et Julian entre dans « the world of guilt and sorrow »), mais « A View of the Woods » nous laisse seulement avec le doute (« This ought to teach you a good lesson, » se dit-il après avoir tué sa petite-fille, mais sa voix « was edged with doubt », 355) – une interrogation que le lecteur peut choisir de laisser ouverte.

Au moment du meurtre, les deux protagonistes sont inextricablement liés représentant les deux facettes indissociables d'une même réalité et lorsqu'ils changent de positions, ils évoquent les figures d'un jeu de cartes où un seul corps divisé est prolongé par un même visage en haut et en bas :

> With a sudden surge of strength, he managed to roll over and reverse their positions so that he was looking down into the face that was his own but had dared to call itself Pitts. (355)

La syntaxe de Flannery O'Connor épouse en partie cette construction en miroir : « Pale identical eye looked into pale identical eye » (355). On notera dans cette formulation l'usage du singulier générique qui universalise l'expérience particulière des deux personnages. Lorsque Mary ne bouge plus, Mr. Fortune « continued to stare at his own conquered image » (355). Il croit avoir tué le Mal qui était hors de lui, il a éradiqué le Bien qui était en lui. Mais la petite fille, elle aussi, est morte d'avoir choisi la division. À un seul bref moment de sa vie, elle a connu un point d'équilibre : lorsqu'elle se définissait comme Mary Fortune-Pitts. Avant, elle n'était que « pure Fortune » et après « pure Pitts » et ce choix de l'incomplétude ne pouvait que lui être fatal. Quant au vieil homme, si O'Connor ne lui avait pas octroyé une mort soudaine sous forme de crise cardiaque, il aurait poursuivi son existence, comme bien des anti-héros modernes, avec le sentiment d'être irrémédiablement divisé.

Horizontalité et verticalité

La division est également le moteur de la narration dans « The Lame Shall Enter First » et elle fonctionne à deux niveaux : horizontal et vertical. Cette nouvelle peut aussi parfaitement se lire sans le secours d'une interprétation religieuse, ce qui ne nous empêche pas d'essayer de comprendre les implications métaphysiques qu'O'Connor souhaite introduire dans son texte.

Le récit est divisé en deux parties qui se situent, pour l'essentiel, dans deux lieux différents : la cuisine et le grenier, ce qui correspond à une structuration verticale de l'espace. Mais chaque lieu est également le siège d'une thématique de la division qui opère cette fois sur le plan horizontal. Les premiers mots de la nouvelle mettent clairement ce motif en place : « Sheppard sat on a stool at the bar *that divided the kitchen in half* » (445, c'est moi qui souligne). Dans cette cuisine, il y a deux personnes que tout devrait rapprocher, mais qu'en réalité tout sépare : le père et le fils, seuls dans la maison depuis la mort de la mère. Au début du récit, ils se trouvent de part et d'autre du comptoir qui divise la cuisine. Le père observe son fils, Norton, d'un œil critique. L'enfant, lui, ne semble pas complètement présent (« the child looked at him *with a kind of half attention,* his eyes forward but not engaged », 445, c'est moi qui souligne). Son visage semble être une réplique de celui de son père, mais en plus pale, comme s'il était menacé d'extinction, à l'instar du cow-boy délavé qui orne son T-shirt. Norton est un enfant triste qui passe la plupart de son temps seul depuis la mort de sa mère et comble le manque en absorbant de la nourriture ou en accumulant de l'argent. Sheppard, lui, est un travailleur social qui remplit le vide de son existence en aidant de jeunes délinquants. Et lorsque le récit débute, il veut convaincre son fils, qu'il juge égoïste, de la nécessité de partager ce qu'il possède avec d'autres enfants plus défavorisés (« share », « divide »). Leur logique de compensation et de substitution trouve ses racines dans le même mal : la solitude et le manque d'amour, mais ils ne peuvent s'entraider car Sheppard est aveuglé par la conviction de sa supériorité intellectuelle et par son besoin de contrôle sur son entourage. Se prenant pour une sorte de Christ laïc, il veut faire le bien des autres contre leur gré. Lorsque Norton comprend que son père entend lui substituer un autre enfant, en la personne du délinquant au pied bot Rufus Johnson, il vomit la nourriture ingurgitée, sans doute dans un ultime appel à la compassion que son père ignore, dégoûté par cette « half-digested food » qui gît dans son assiette et qui lui rend son fils encore plus haïssable. Lorsque Rufus Johnson pénètre effectivement dans la maison en l'absence de Sheppard, il dépossède Norton de tous ses repères et va jusqu'à souiller le dernier sanctuaire où le petit garçon trouvait refuge : la chambre de sa mère. Celle-ci est décrite comme plongée dans une « semi-darkness » avec une énorme coiffeuse dont le miroir brille « in the half light ». Toutes ces demi-teintes associées au sentiment d'incomplétude et de vide qui caractérisent Norton suggèrent que son monde s'est brisé en deux à la mort de sa mère. Or son père, loin de remédier à cet état de chose, le renforce en déclarant :

> "*We need another boy in the house.*" There was a genuine desperation in his voice. "Norton here has *never had to divide anything in his life. He does not know what it means to share.* And I need somebody to teach him. How about helping me out ? Stay here for a while with us, Rufus. I need your help." The excitement in his voice made it thin. (457, c'est moi qui souligne)

Après avoir perdu sa mère, Norton perd donc maintenant son père et son univers s'écroule définitivement. Dans la maison divisée dont il doit partager le salon tous les soirs avec Rufus, d'autres séparations peu à peu se dessinent. Rufus se déclare possédé par Satan et Sheppard, intellectuel athée et rationaliste, décide de lui faire découvrir les vertus de la science. Il installe donc au sommet de la maison, dans le grenier, un télescope et un microscope pour l'initier aux beautés de l'infiniment grand et de l'infiniment petit. Il lui parle des astronautes et espère ainsi remplacer les croyances créationnistes de Rufus par de saines théories évolutionnistes. La maison est donc divisée à présent verticalement en deux lieux : celui du rez-de-chaussée où se passe la vie matérielle quotidienne et celui du grenier où s'affrontent deux conceptions du monde et deux manières d'être « sauvé ». Mais Rufus résiste à l'enseignement que lui prodigue généreusement Sheppard et s'ingénie à lui démontrer qu'il ne connaît que le Mal. Norton est donc de plus en plus négligé par son père qui le laisse plus que jamais seul à la maison (« He left Norton at home because *he did not want his attention divided* », 469, c'est moi qui souligne). Par un renversement inattendu des choses, le petit garçon se met à s'intéresser à la religion car Rufus l'a convaincu que sa mère était au ciel et qu'il pourrait la rejoindre lorsqu'il mourrait. À la fin, les configurations initiales de l'espace sont elles aussi renversées. Norton passe son temps dans le grenier à examiner la lune et les étoiles. Rufus, arrêté par la police, retourne en maison de correction et Sheppard se retrouve seul dans la cuisine où Norton au début essayait vainement de trouver des palliatifs au manque d'attention dont il souffrait. À ce stade, le père prend enfin conscience de son égoïsme et du peu d'intérêt qu'il a manifesté à son fils depuis l'arrivée de Rufus dans la maison. Pris de remords, il monte le rejoindre, mais trop tard : il le trouve pendu à l'une des poutres du grenier car l'enfant, en mourant, a voulu retrouver sa mère au paradis.

Dans la logique de Flannery O'Connor, cette ultime scène de réconciliation dans le grenier, même si elle arrive à un moment où elle ne peut plus apporter à Sheppard que des regrets éternels, est censée l'amener sur la voie d'une révélation teilhardienne. Il découvre non seulement qu'esprit et matière ne sauraient être divisés, mais également que science et foi peuvent être réconciliés[1]. Si cette idée

1 Voir André Daleux, *Teilhard de Chardin : Science et foi réconciliées ?* Paris : Ed. Gabriandre, 2001.

était incompatible avec les conceptions de la science au XIXe siècle, en revanche, au XXe, les découvertes des physiques quantique et relativiste ont profondément modifié le paysage scientifique, introduisant en particulier une possibilité d'incertitude et de mystère. Les « relations d'incertitudes » définies par Werner Heisenberg disent l'impossibilité de connaître toutes les données d'une particule quantique, et cela d'autant plus que l'on ignore la manière dont les résultats scientifiques sont tributaires de l'expérience, voire de la présence de l'observateur. Tout ceci, bien évidemment, mine les notions de déterminisme absolu et de totale fiabilité de la relation de cause à effet sur lesquelles la physique classique reposait. Max Planck ira même jusqu'à envisager « une réalité métaphysique » à l'horizon du réel expérimental. À cela s'est ajouté le fameux $E = MC^2$ d'Einstein qui ne définit plus la matière comme solide et inerte, mais comme une énergie où la masse d'un corps varie avec sa vitesse de déplacement et l'écoulement de son temps propre.

Teilhard de Chardin, jésuite de formation scientifique, s'est donc saisi de ces nouvelles données pour remettre en question, non seulement l'opposition entre esprit et matière mais aussi entre causalité et finalité. Sa théologie cosmique ou « noogenèse » défend l'idée que recherche scientifique, vision théologique et philosophie morale se rejoignent, car elle s'appuie sur le principe « anthropique » qui voit dans la formation des structures complexes de l'univers un processus d'évolution qui va de la matière la plus élémentaire à l'organisation la plus subtile de la pensée. Le but de l'univers serait l'homme et la complexité de sa conscience, ce mouvement culminant dans ce que Teilhard de Chardin appelle le « Point Omega ». Pour lui, cet état final « superhumain » serait celui de la reconnaissance de la présence de l'esprit dans la matière, c'est-à-dire de l'incarnation du Christ dans le monde, mais cette trajectoire où tout « converge » ne serait pas linéaire. Comme les scientifiques qui pensent qu'il a fallu une synchronisation étonnante de phénomènes physiques (« fine tuning ») pour produire le cosmos, il faut des conditions parfois extraordinaires pour parvenir à une telle révélation. Et celle-ci ne s'obtient que par un double mouvement actif/passif, c'est-à-dire à la fois grâce à une volonté d'agir sur le monde mais aussi par une acceptation des épreuves qui nous sont imposées. Cette dynamique se résume dans un désir de croissance ou de « surcréation », mais aussi dans une humilité qui refuse l'égoïsme et la volonté de puissance. Il s'agit de repousser au plus loin ses limites à l'intérieur de l'espace qu'il nous a été donné d'occuper en ce monde, ce que le père Teilhard exprime ainsi :

> Il n'y a pour chacun de nous, à chaque instant, qu'une seule place possible, celle où nous établit la fidélité continuée aux devoirs naturels et surnaturels de la vie. En ce point, auquel nous ne nous trouvons au moment voulu que si nous déployons, sur tous les terrains, notre plus industrieuse activité, Dieu se communiquera à nous dans sa plénitude.[1]

Par ailleurs, le théologien considère que « nous constituons chacun un centre particulier de divinisation (en sorte qu'il y a autant de Milieux divins partiels que d'âmes chrétiennes) ».[2] C'est cette théologie, qui elle-même s'exprime par des métaphores spatiales, que Flannery O'Connor s'efforce de mettre en scène (et en espace) dans ses nouvelles. On voit donc toute l'importance pour elle de créer des centres de conscience dont la vision du monde est nécessairement bornée et d'examiner la manière dont ces « îlots » entrent (ou non) en interaction avec d'autres centres de conscience et avec la portion du monde qui leur est donné d'occuper. D'où le choix de la focalisation interne qui place le lecteur aux côtés du personnage et lui fait voir les choses par ses yeux. D'où également les changements de focalisation qui peuvent avoir lieu à l'intérieur de certaines nouvelles et qui montrent la juxtaposition de ces univers intérieurs. Ainsi, dans « Good Country People », la narration oscille-t-elle entre le point de vue de Mrs. Hopewell et celui de Joy/Hulga, comme dans « The Displaced Person » celui de Mrs. Shortley est remplacé, à partir du deuxième « acte » de cette tragédie, par celui de Mrs. McIntyre. Dans « Everything That Rises Must Converge » la focalisation est centrée de bout en bout sur le personnage de Julian, mais lui-même est conscient que sa mère évolue dans un univers parallèle au sien qu'il peut imaginer, mais auquel il n'a pas accès :

> Behind the newspaper Julian was withdrawing into the inner compartment of his mind where he spent most of his time. This was a kind of mental bubble in which he established himself when he could not bear to be a part of what was going on around him. From it he could see out and judge but in it he was safe from any kind of penetration from without. It was the only place where he felt free of the general idiocy of his fellows. His mother had never entered it but from it he could see her with absolute clarity. […]
> She lived according to the laws of her own fantasy world, outside of which he had never seen her set foot. (411)

---

1 Teilhard de Chardin, *Le Milieu divin*, Paris : Seuil, 1957, p. 142.
2 *Op. cit.*, p. 165.

Cette logique d'enfermement des personnages à l'intérieur des compartiments de leur vie intérieure est assez caractéristique de toute la littérature des années 1950. La thématique de la solitude et de l'incommunicabilité se retrouve en particulier dans le « théâtre de l'absurde ». On peut penser ici aux pièces d'Edward Albee, en particulier *The Zoo Story* où l'isolement du protagoniste est figuré par le cloisonnement des multiples chambres de l'hôtel où il loge et où tout le monde se croise et s'ignore. On songe également à l'enfermement à l'intérieur de la prison d'un langage stéréotypé chez Beckett ou chez Ionesco, deux auteurs qui viennent immédiatement à l'esprit lorsqu'on lit les collections de clichés de Mrs. Hopewell et de Mrs. Freeman dans « Good Country People ». Quant aux jeunes intellectuels murés dans leur silence et leur morosité, ils semblent voir le monde à travers une cloche de verre comme s'ils sortaient tout droit du roman de Sylvia Plath du même nom (*The Bell Jar*).

Ce qui différencie O'Connor des écrivains de sa génération, c'est donc la thématique de la verticalité et de la convergence. En dehors des strates de la maison de Sheppard, où la révélation a lieu bien sûr au sommet, cette thématique apparaît sous forme d'images d'échelles célestes que les protagonistes voient soudain se profiler sur un horizon nuageux, mais que les moins éclairés d'entre eux confondent (comme Mrs. Turpin au début de « Revelation ») avec l'échelle sociale. Car pour s'élever jusqu'à la vision divine, il faut renoncer à ses privilèges, faire l'expérience du dépouillement et de la dépossession et surtout, il faut savoir déchiffrer les symboles correctement – c'est-à-dire repérer, dans le monde, les signes qui témoignent de la présence de l'Esprit dans la création.

10

Des forêts de symboles

La nature est un temple où de vivants piliers
Laissent parfois sortir de confuses paroles.
L'homme y passe à travers des forêts de symboles
Qui l'observent avec des regards familiers.

Baudelaire, *Correspondances.*

Tout est symbole chez Flannery O'Connor, mais rien n'est facilement interprétable car toute perception est filtrée par un centre de conscience qui interpose sa propre compréhension des choses (souvent limitée) et fait écran entre le lecteur et le texte. Il n'en reste pas moins qu'on peut admettre que, chez elle comme chez Baudelaire, de mystérieuses « correspondances » existent entre le monde sensible et le monde des Idées ou de l'Esprit. Et à l'instar du poète français, la romancière américaine fait de la nature le topos privilégié de l'interface matière/esprit, même si une révélation peut toujours se produire par d'autres biais.

Dans les nouvelles, la nature est effectivement un temple dont les piliers semblent vivants. Au début de « A View of the Woods », une rangée d'arbres, à l'horizon, semble marcher sur l'eau du lac artificiel que l'on vient de creuser et, à la fin, le personnage central, écrasé par l'acte monstrueux qu'il vient de commettre (le meurtre de sa petite-fille) a une vision de ces mêmes arbres marchant toujours sur l'eau mais s'éloignant de lui :

> On both sides of him he saw that the gaunt trees had thickened into mysterious dark files that were marching across the water and away into the distance. He looked around desperately for someone to help him but the place was deserted except for one huge yellow monster which sat to the side, as stationary as he was, gorging itself on clay. (356)

Un peu plus tôt dans le texte, ces arbres, au soleil couchant, évoquent immanquablement, à travers des images répétées de blessures (« the red light that gushed from the almost hidden sun », « as if someone were wounded [...] and the trees were bathed in blood », 348), le martyre du Christ. Cette symbolique assez évidente n'est pourtant pas perçue par le personnage qui se croit victime d'une « hallucination ». Pire encore, il leur donne une signification tout à fait opposée, puisqu'il les qualifie de « hellish red trunks » (348). Ce jeu d'oppositions n'est possible que parce que le texte opère un va-et-vient entre les commentaires d'un narrateur extérieur et la vision intériorisée du protagoniste. O'Connor, on le sait, était consciente que, dans leur grande majorité, ses lecteurs étaient athées ou sceptiques. Pourtant, ici, elle table sur leur connaissance des textes religieux pour comprendre la dynamique de son œuvre. Ou alors, il faut imaginer que, sans cette connaissance de base, le lecteur se retrouve dans la même situation que le personnage et que le récit perd sa dimension symbolique pour se réduire à un conflit psychologique. Pourtant, en nous disant que Mr. Fortune voit dans les arbres rougeoyants une image de l'Enfer, O'Connor nous installe bien *explicitement* dans une symbolique religieuse dont son protagoniste ne perçoit que le côté négatif. Et, puisque ce dernier est construit progressivement comme quelqu'un qui s'aveugle sur lui-même et sur le désir des autres, le lecteur est donc invité à corriger l'image erronée que ce personnage se fait des symboles qui lui sont proposés. Est-ce ainsi que l'écrivain espérait faire glisser doucement le lecteur athée vers une interprétation christique qui deviendrait satisfaisante pour l'esprit dans la mesure où elle serait associée à une version positive du personnage, ouvert aux aspirations de son entourage et défenseur de la nature ?

Les autres nouvelles abondent en protagonistes athées auxquels le lecteur non-croyant peut être tenté de s'identifier dans un premier temps. Surtout lorsque ce sont des intellectuels dont il partage la critique d'une société aux préjugés bien ancrés. Mais O'Connor ne lui laisse pas longtemps cette satisfaction. En forçant le trait et en montrant les conséquences *humaines* dommageables que ces individus infligent à leurs proches par leur froideur et leur égoïsme, elle prévient tout désir de s'identifier plus avant. Et le lecteur mécréant se retrouve dans une situation très inconfortable où il n'a plus de repères auxquels se raccrocher. Car, sans parler d'identification véritable, il cherche au moins une position philosophique à laquelle il pourrait adhérer, or celle-ci ne lui est proposée ni par les personnages ni par le narrateur. Est-ce à dire que l'on ne peut pas lire O'Connor si l'on ne partage pas ses croyances et si l'on refuse son système symbolique figé ?

Nous avons vu qu'il était possible de faire une lecture non religieuse de « A View of the Woods » en s'arrêtant simplement sur le doute qui s'insinue dans l'esprit du héros et sans chercher à saturer immédiatement ce doute de sens. En fait, on pourrait même avancer que l'abondance des signes symboliques dans le texte induit une défiance généralisée vis-à-vis de leur signification et que le lecteur termine le plus souvent le récit « saturated in depression », comme Julian dans « Everything that Rises Must Converge » que touché par une épiphanie. C'est là l'un des paradoxes de ces textes et l'on peut se demander si O'Connor en était consciente. Toujours est-il qu'à part quelques images récurrentes comme celle du soleil couchant qui évoque le Christ souffrant ou la ligne de bois sombres à l'horizon qui suggère le mystère de la création (divine), la plupart des autres symboles sont plus fluctuants et peuvent se charger d'une pluralité de sens, ou du moins de différentes strates de sens qui ne s'annulent pas en s'accumulant.

The Machine in the Garden

On peut faire plusieurs lectures symboliques de l'utilisation de la nature dans les nouvelles. Pour rester dans « A View of the Woods », on notera que, dès les premiers paragraphes, une série d'hypallages produisent différents effets : soit celui d'une réification de la nature (« The red corrugated lake », 335), soit celui d'une naturalisation de la machine (« a battered mulberry-colored Cadillac », 335). La signification de l'interpénétration entre les deux mondes (naturel et mécanique) semble d'abord brouillée, mais se précise au troisième paragraphe où la machine est clairement décrite comme monstrueuse et destructrice pour la nature (« the big disembodied gullet gorge itself on clay », 335).

Cette nouvelle présente trois conceptions de la nature : la « wilderness », figurée par la forêt sombre et mystérieuse ; la Pastorale, typifiée par « the cow pasture » et la nature recréée par la machine, représentée par le lac artificiel. Ces trois conceptions renvoient à une problématique récurrente dans la littérature et la culture américaines.

On y voit la Pastorale Jeffersonienne prise en étau entre deux dangers, celui du retour à la nature sauvage d'un côté et celui de la mécanisation (et de l'urbanisation) à outrance de l'autre. C'est aussi une problématique plus particulièrement sudiste puisque cette région a été industrialisée plus tardivement que le Nord.

Mais, dès le départ, ces différentes notions étaient teintées de connotations religieuses, que l'on retrouve ici légèrement modifiées. La Pastorale correspond au jardin d'Eden après la chute. C'est celui dans lequel le Mal a été introduit et où Adam doit reconstruire son paradis à la sueur de son front. Cette idée est suggérée ici par le fait que Pitts, le père de Mary, avait réussi à éradiquer toutes les mauvaises herbes du « cow pasture » avant que Mr. Fortune ne le vende. La « wilderness » peut être perçue positivement ou négativement, selon que l'on définisse la nature à l'état brut comme le chaos informe des origines, menaçant et dangereux, ou comme le paradis avant la chute, berceau bienveillant du Bon Sauvage. Chez O'Connor c'est avant tout le lieu du mystère, celui de l'incarnation, qui se pare de connotations positives ou négatives suivant le point de vue de l'observateur. La nature transformée par la machine participe du monstrueux, du difforme. C'est une sorte de « freak ». Mais comme, pour Flannery O'Connor, la révélation de la présence divine peut être induite par son absence criante, le monstre sera éventuellement l'agent d'une prise de conscience. On remarquera également que le nouvel Adam de cette histoire, celui qui s'applique à pourchasser le Mal dans la nature, s'appelle Pitts ce qui devrait, en théorie, l'associer aux abîmes de l'Enfer – preuve s'il en est que les symboles doivent être maniés avec précaution.

Tout symbole peut se retourner en son contraire. C'est la leçon que l'on peut tirer de l'onomastique dans cette histoire comme dans d'autres. Et il en est de même pour la symbolique des couleurs.

La symbolique des couleurs

Dans ce domaine, certains symboles sont figés et se retrouvent d'une nouvelle à l'autre. C'est le cas, bien évidemment pour les couleurs rouges et violettes, en général associées au soleil couchant, aux arbres ou à l'eau (dans « The River ») et qui le plus souvent figurent les souffrances et le sang du Christ.

Le soleil cependant n'est pas toujours rouge, et lorsqu'il est pâle ou d'un blanc aveuglant, il peut soit représenter une menace, soit être le corrélat objectif de l'aveuglement du personnage (ou les deux à la fois). Dans « Greenleaf », Mrs. May fait un rêve proleptique où le soleil joue un rôle déterminant :

> She became aware after a time that the noise was *the sun trying to burn through the tree line* and she stopped to watch, safe in the knowledge that it couldn't, that it had to sink the way it always did outside of her property. When she first stopped *it was a swollen red ball,* but as she stood watching *it began to narrow and pale until it looked like a bullet.* Then suddenly *it burst through the tree line* and raced down the hill toward her. (329, c'est moi qui souligne)

Cette vision du soleil qui la transperce annonce sa crucifixion finale, immolée par ses ennemis, ou du moins par le taureau « aux longues jambes » qui en est la métaphore. L'image de la balle de fusil est, en revanche, plus insolite, car elle ne semble pas entrer dans un champ lexical cohérent avec celui de l'animalité ou de la nature suggéré par les images précédentes. Elle était pourtant déjà apparue un peu plus tôt dans le récit, toujours associée au soleil pale :

> The metal stanchions gleamed ferociously and she had to squint to be able to look at all. She drew her head out of the room quickly and closed the door and leaned against it, frowning. The light outside was not so bright but she was conscious that the sun was directly on top of her head, like a silver bullet ready to drop into her brain. (325)

La scène se passe lorsque Mrs. May est allée chez O.T. et E.T. Greenleaf pour leur demander d'enfermer le taureau qui détruit sa maison et menace d'abâtardir son troupeau. En l'absence des deux jeunes gens, elle explore leur laiterie et ne peut s'empêcher d'être éblouie (au sens propre comme au sens figuré) par la propreté et la modernité des lieux. Cette vision redouble sa conviction que les frères Greenleaf s'apprêtent à causer sa ruine, puisqu'ils la concurrencent sur son propre terrain. En effet, elle aussi possède une laiterie comme la leur, mais beaucoup moins bien équipée et surtout beaucoup moins mécanisée. La réussite des deux garçons est due à la guerre au cours de laquelle ils ont été blessés, ce qui leur a valu une pension et des subventions de l'État pour installer cette ferme modèle. L'image, apparemment saugrenue, de la balle de fusil, se justifie donc ici par ce double renvoi à un monde de violence et à un univers dominé par la machine. La balle, qui, selon la logique déterministe de Mrs May, aurait dû faire disparaître les frères

Greenleaf (placés au bas de l'échelle sociale), a au contraire permis leur succès « contre-nature » et se retourne à présent contre elle pour l'exterminer. Et la blancheur aveuglante du soleil vient souligner à la fois son sens de la menace et son refus de voir (ou d'admettre) les changements qui sont en train de s'opérer dans la société. À la fin, si Mrs. May n'est pas tuée par la balle d'une arme moderne mais par un taureau (élément « naturel »), c'est aussi à cause de la non-intervention de Mr. Greenleaf qui utilise trop tard son fusil pour abattre la bête. Il s'agit donc d'un « meurtre passif » au cours duquel l'employé de Mrs. May se tient en retrait pour laisser s'accomplir le Destin qui instaure un nouvel ordre social, ordre qui vient se substituer à celui que Mrs. May a connu et que « la nouvelle société » considèrera bientôt comme « naturel » (les noms O.T et E.T. pourraient d'ailleurs signifier « Ouest » et « Est », ce qui est suggéré par le geste de leur employé noir lorsqu'il veut les localiser : « pointing first to the left and then to the right as if he were naming the position of two planets », 325). Auparavant, la réussite des frères Greenleaf avait déjà été décrite par Mrs. May à l'aide de formules actives/passives (« The smartest thing *they had done was to get sent* overseas and there to marry French wives. », « They *had both managed to get wounded* and now they both had pensions. », 318) – formulations qui, de son point de vue, laissaient entendre que les frères Greenleaf avaient manipulé le Destin à leur avantage, mais admettaient aussi indirectement que ce Destin était à présent en marche et que rien se saurait l'arrêter.

Dans cette nouvelle, la couleur dominante est le vert. On la trouve d'emblée dans le nom des personnages qui donnent son titre au récit. Accolée au feuillage, elle évoque une nature qu'on pourrait penser idyllique et paradisiaque. Mais, comme l'Eden, elle peut être envisagée aussi bien comme un symbole d'innocence que de chute, et offre donc une double face selon le point de vue de la personne qui focalise le récit. Dans de nombreuses nouvelles, la couleur verte signale la présence d'une personne démoniaque, ou jugée démoniaque par les autres personnages, ce qui n'est pas la même chose puisque la symbolique peut se renverser au cours du récit. D'ailleurs, cette couleur est souvent associée à des teintes dorées, ce qui renvoie alors aux « soleils » qui illuminent la roue du paon en qui, on le sait, Flannery O'Connor, à l'instar du prêtre catholique de « The Displaced Person », voyait une image du Christ incarné :

> "So beauti-ful," the priest said. "A tail full of suns," and he crept forward on tiptoe and looked down on the bird's back where the polished *gold and green* design began. The peacock stood still as if he had just come down from some sun-drenched height to be a vision for them all. The priest's homely red face hung over him, glowing with pleasure. (198) [...]
> The priest let his eyes wander toward the birds. They had reached the middle of the lawn. They stopped suddenly and curving his neck backwards, he raised his tail and spread it with a shimmering timbrous noise. *Tiers of small pregnant suns floated in a green-gold haze* over his head. The priest stood transfixed, his jaw slack. Mrs. McIntyre wondered where she had ever seen such an idiotic old man. *"Christ will come like that!"* he said in a loud gay voice and wiped his hand over his mouth and stood there, gaping. (226, c'est moi qui souligne)

Ici, l'admiration du prêtre pour les plumes de paon vertes et dorées n'est pas partagée par Mrs. McIntyre qui trouve le vieil homme « idiot ». Or, quelques phrases plus loin, l'« expression puritaine » de la fermière nous renseigne sur les véritables raisons de ce jugement négatif. Elle est protestante et, ne souhaitant pas se laisser influencer par les croyances du prêtre, elle reste hermétique à tout jugement de valeur de sa part. L'interprétation symbolique des couleurs témoignant de l'enfermement des personnages dans un système de références personnel, il n'est donc pas étonnant que, lorsque Mrs. Shortley voit le Polonais pour la première fois, elle note immédiatement ses « little green eyes » (197) qu'elle choisira plus tard de déchiffrer comme un signe de son appartenance au démon.

Dans « A Sroke of Good Fortune », la couleur verte des « collard greens » est associée à tout ce que Ruby, la jeune femme placée au centre du récit, a rejeté depuis longtemps et en particulier le village de son enfance dont le nom, « Pitman », suffit à évoquer le caractère arriéré et, pour elle, démoniaque. Là encore, l'onomastique nous montre qu'elle n'a pas vraiment échappé à ses origines puisqu'elle a épousé un garçon, Bill Hill, dont le nom lui aussi fleure bon la campagne (malgré ses airs de citadins, il est resté un « hill billy », un bouseux). Dans la cage d'escalier de son immeuble, tout son passé lui revient en écho, sous forme de métaphores colorées :

> She looked down into *the stairwell* and gave a long hollow wail that widened and *echoed* as it went down. *The stair cavern was dark green and mole-colored* and the wail sounded at the very bottom like *a voice answering her*. (106)

Cet escalier, décrit comme « a stairwell » ou « a stair cavern », n'est pas très différent de la fosse, du trou perdu (« pit ») de son enfance. D'autant plus que ses murs sont peints en vert. Mais ils sont aussi caractérisés par une autre nuance plus inhabituelle : la couleur « taupe ». Dans cette nouvelle de jeunesse, où la symbolique est plus grossière, on aura compris d'emblée que cette image animale est censée représenter son aveuglement.

Dans « A Good man is Hard to Find », le vert est d'abord la couleur du foulard ridicule de la belle-fille de l'héroïne, dont le visage par ailleurs est aussi associé à un légume :

> [The grandmother] wheeled around then and faced the children's mother, a young woman in slacks, whose face was *as broad and innocent as a cabbage* and was tied around with *a green head-kerchief* that had two points on the top *like a rabbit's ears*. (117)

Si l'image veut suggérer ici, de manière assez naïve, l'innocence d'une nature édénique, plus tard l'idée sera battue en brèche par la femme de Red Sammy qui assure ne voir sur terre que le Mal :

> "It isn't a soul in this green world of God's that you can trust," she said. "And I don't count nobody out of that, not nobody," she repeated, looking at Red Sammy.
> "Did you read about that criminal, The Misfit, that's escaped ?" asked the grandmother. (122)

Le regard de la femme en direction de Red Sam au moment de la remarque de la grand-mère sur le « Désaxé » semble insinuer qu'une parenté pourrait être établie entre les deux, lien possible qui est renforcé par la ressemblance de Sammy avec les acolytes du meurtrier (qui n'en sont eux-mêmes que l'image redoublée) : il porte un pantalon kaki comme l'un d'entre eux et il est gros et pousse de temps en temps une tyrolienne comme l'autre. Les vêtements empruntés des trois hommes en font, de toute façon, une représentation composite d'êtres humains, tous semblables et interchangeables.

Le décor du restaurant/station service de Red Sam ressemble aussi étrangement à celui de Tilman dans la nouvelle « A View of the Wood », Tilman dont les yeux verts et le visage triangulaire évoque explicitement le serpent dans le jardin :

> He sat habitually with his arms folded on the counter and his insignificant head *weaving snake-fashion* above them. He had *a triangular-shaped face* with the point at the bottom and the top of his skull was covered with a cap of freckles. *His eyes were green* and very narrow and *his tongue was always exposed* in his partly opened mouth. (352, c'est moi qui souligne)

« Le Serpent dans le Jardin » est également une formule interchangeable avec « La Machine dans le jardin », puisque, dans les deux histoires, la mort est associée à l'automobile. En effet, Tilman cache, derrière les aspects avenants de son établissement, un cimetière de voitures et un magasin de pierres tombales :

> Tilman's was bordered on either side by a field of *used-car bodies*, a kind of ward for *incurable automobiles*. He also sold outdoor ornaments, such as *stone cranes and chickens*, urns, jardinières, whirligigs, and farther back from the road, so as not to depress his dance-hall customers, *a line of tombstones and monuments*. (345, c'est moi qui souligne)

On notera dans cette dernière description la présence de la même pétrification du vivant ou personnification de la machine (par le biais de divers hypallages) que dans le début de la nouvelle – le tout baignant dans une atmosphère mortifère de maladie terminale (« incurable »).

Mrs. Connin de « The River » est dotée d'une apparence physique qui, elle aussi, allie la mort à la nature verdoyante : « a speckled *skeleton* in a long *pea-green* coat and felt helmet » (157, c'est moi qui souligne). Quant à la forêt que le petit garçon traverse avec elle pour se rendre à la rivière, c'est un lieu nouveau pour lui et il est parsemé d'éléments colorés à la symbolique ambivalente, c'est-à-dire à la fois beaux et inquiétants :

> They walked on the dirt road for a while and then they crossed a field stippled with *purple weeds* and entered *the shadows of a wood* where the ground was covered with thick pine needles. *He had never been in woods before* and he walked carefully, looking from side to side *as if he were entering a strange country*. They moved along a bridle path that twisted downhill through *crackling red leaves*, and once, catching at a branch to keep himself from slipping, he looked into *two frozen green-gold eyes enclosed in the darkness* of a tree hole. At the bottom of the hill, the woods opened suddenly onto a pasture dotted here and there with *black and white cows* and sloping down, tier after tier, to *a broad orange stream* where the reflection of the sun was set *like a diamond*. (164, c'est moi qui souligne)

Dans « A Circle in the Fire », l'univers protégé de l'enfant se compose de champs et de prairies (« the fields were a patchwork of gray and yellow greens », 176) que sa mère, nous l'avons vu, s'occupe de débarrasser de leurs mauvaises herbes, abritée du soleil sous un chapeau d'un vert éclatant (« bright green », 175). Lorsque cet univers est menacé par l'intrusion des trois garçons, le soleil prend des teintes de feu et les pâturages perdent leur aspect familier et rassurant (« the grass was an unnatural green as if it were turning to glass », 185). À la fin, la couleur verte se pare d'une signification ambiguë, car elle nous est présentée à travers la projection du regard de la fillette qui essaie d'imaginer ce que voit Powell (« the trees must have looked like green waterfalls through his wet glasses »,

191-192). Il est difficile alors de savoir exactement à qui attribuer cette perception d'une nature luxuriante. Peut-être faut-il y voir l'expression de deux nostalgies qui se superposent : l'une (celle du garçon) pour la disparition de ce monde pastoral idéalisé qu'il aurait voulu s'approprier et va, à défaut, faire partir en fumée ; l'autre (celle de la petite fille) pour la perte irrémédiable de son innocence, symbolisée par le viol de son sanctuaire et la vision des garçons nus.

À la fin de « A Temple of the Holy Ghost », la couleur verte signe aussi la fin de l'innocence et la découverte de la sexualité (« a stretch of pasture land that rose and fell with a gathering greenness », 248). Celle-ci a été amenée par le récit de l'hermaphrodite exhibant ses organes génitaux dans une tente de foire. Dans l'esprit de la fillette, cette vision se superpose à celle de l'élévation de l'hostie qui prend alors un tour bien païen. Mais, pour Flannery O'Connor, les deux ne sont pas incompatibles. La dernière image, par exemple, peut se lire à travers une symbolique religieuse aussi bien que sexuelle, la ligne ensanglantée qui se dessine sur le ciel après l'élévation suggérant une défloration :

> The sun was a huge red ball like an elevated Host drenched in blood and when it sank out of sight, it left a line in the sky like a clay road hanging over the trees. (248)

La lecture religieuse de la révélation est cependant déjà introduite quelques paragraphes plus tôt à travers la description des couleurs de la chapelle : « The chapel smelled of incense. It was light green and gold » (247). L'or renvoie au soleil et à une conception transcendante de Dieu ; le vert renvoie à la nature (dont la sexualité fait partie) et à une conception immanente du Divin.

Métaphores et métonymies

La métaphore est un déplacement de sens d'un mot à un autre, reposant sur une analogie sous-entendue. La métonymie consiste à désigner une chose par un élément avec lequel cette chose entretient une relation nécessaire (l'effet par la cause, le contenu par le contenant, le tout par la partie etc.). La métonymie sépare, divise, isole des caractéristiques d'un même objet. La métaphore superpose, empile, rajoute des couches de sens. La métonymie réduit l'objet à l'une de ses fonctions, la métaphore l'enrichit d'échos qui peuvent être très variés. On aura compris donc que la métonymie fonctionne essentiellement sur un mode horizontal et sera utilisée par O'Connor pour représenter le monde divisé des non-croyants ou des mauvais chrétiens, alors que la métaphore opère sur le mode vertical et lui servira à rendre l'élargissement de la vision que procure la révélation divine.

Métaphores

Certaines métaphores sont figées parce qu'empruntées à la Bible, ou plus généralement à des références classiques de la culture occidentale. La croix, le jardin, le berger (Sheppard dans « The Lame Shall Enter First »), le serpent, le feu, le gouffre, le ciel etc. sont des métaphores chrétiennes classiques. Certaines autres sont empruntées à la mythologie (le taureau/Zeus) ou à la littérature (les cercles de l'Enfer chez Dante). Certaines, en revanche, appartiennent à l'univers familier de Flannery O'Connor : le paon, les buses qui se posent en haut des arbres, les bois sombres ou rougeoyants sur la ligne d'horizon, les maladies ou difformités, la voiture maléfique…

L'image du cercle, dont nous avons noté la récurrence lorsque nous avons étudié la structuration de l'espace, peut se concevoir comme une description littérale (Mr. Guizac fauche effectivement les blés en décrivant des cercles concentriques autour de la tombe du Juge) ou comme une métaphore. Mais, dans cette dernière fonction, elle peut avoir plusieurs significations. Elle peut figurer la prise de pouvoir progressive de Mr. Guizac qui se rapproche de plus en plus du centre occupé par l'ancien propriétaire des lieux comme s'il voulait prendre sa place. Or, puisque le centre est présenté par ailleurs comme spirituellement vide, elle peut aussi dénoncer la vanité de cette quête matérielle, suggérant donc que le salut se trouve dans la dépossession, c'est-à-dire non point dans le centre mais dans la périphérie. Ce qui est sans doute l'ultime découverte que fait Mrs. McIntyre. Et enfin, elle peut renvoyer à la conception teilhardienne du « Milieu divin » et figurer le fait que « nous constituons chacun un centre de divinisation »[1] potentiellement capable de converger vers le Point Omega de l'existence en Dieu, mais là encore à condition d'abandonner toute vanité, égoïsme et désir d'appropriation.

La nouvelle « Parker's Back » présente une utilisation très similaire des cercles concentriques. Parker, qui n'est pas croyant mais a

1 *Op. cit.*, p. 165.

épousé une femme puritaine très rigoriste, veut se faire tatouer une image de Dieu dans le dos (le reste de son corps est pratiquement recouvert de tatouages). Il espère ainsi enfin plaire à son épouse qui ne semble jamais apprécier sa conduite. Pour gagner sa vie, Parker travaille dans une ferme possédée par une vieille femme. Un jour, la propriétaire lui demande d'aller ramasser le foin coupé dans un pré au centre duquel se trouve un très vieil arbre qu'elle lui recommande de ne pas endommager avec son tracteur. Comme Mr. Guizac, il ramasse le foin en décrivant des cercles concentriques qui le rapprochent de plus en plus de l'arbre. Pendant qu'il accomplit sa tâche mécaniquement, il pense au tatouage qu'il va choisir et qui devrait enfin lui assurer les bonnes grâces de son épouse. L'esprit ailleurs, il oublie le vieil arbre qu'il heurte par inadvertance et son tracteur prend feu détruisant l'arbre par la même occasion. Penaud, il se sauve au volant de son camion et va en ville se faire faire le tatouage désiré.

Ceci est une façon de raconter l'histoire littéralement et le lecteur peut s'arrêter à ce niveau d'interprétation purement psychologique. Mais dans le contexte religieux qui « encercle » ce récit dans le récit, le lecteur est amené à chercher une autre interprétation. Lorsque l'arbre devient une torche enflammée, Parker, saisi de stupeur, s'écrit « GOD ABOVE ! » et recule en regrettant de ne pas savoir se signer. L'exclamation pourrait n'être qu'un juron, mais l'on pressent qu'il prend pour lui une signification « littérale », la littéralité changeant de camp si l'on fait de la spiritualité la seule vérité de l'être comme le préconisait Teilhard de Chardin. Mais, entre les deux littéralités, matérielle/psychologique d'une part et spirituelle d'autre part, le lien s'est fait par le biais d'un récit enchâssé, comme une parabole biblique, dans lequel l'arbre enflammé devient une métaphore d'une métaphore, celle du buisson ardent qui révèle à Moïse la Présence de Dieu et la mission que ce dernier lui assigne : celle de sauver son peuple. L'ensemble de la nouvelle peut alors se lire comme une réécriture de l'histoire de Moïse fuyant sa famille dont il ne partage pas la religion, épousant une fille de village et devenant berger avant d'avoir, sur la montagne, la révélation divine de son destin.

La métaphore biblique, par ailleurs, s'arrête là. Le reste est le produit de l'imaginaire o'connorien. Et, dans l'univers conçu par l'auteur, le tatouage va prendre peu à peu la valeur d'une métaphore spirituelle. Dans un premier temps, Parker ne faisait tatouer que des objets, puis des animaux, puis des êtres humains, suivant ainsi la chaîne teilhardienne (qui était également la hiérarchie élisabéthaine du monde) allant de la matière inanimée pour converger vers l'humain et trouver son apothéose en Dieu.

Lorsque le Christ byzantin est enfin tatoué dans son dos, Parker n'est pas pressé de le voir et l'artiste doit le forcer à confronter cette image grâce à un jeu de miroirs, mais il ne peut pas soutenir ce regard sur lui (et qui vient, en quelque sorte, de lui) très longtemps :

> Parker looked, turned white and moved away. The eyes in the reflected face continued to look at him – still, straight, all-demanding, enclosed in silence. (525-526)

Plus tard, passant la soirée dans un bar avant de rentrer chez lui, Parker rencontre d'anciens camarades de beuveries qui demandent à voir son dernier tatouage :

> "Come on," the big man said, "let's have a look at O.E.'s tatoo," and Parker squirmed in their hands, they pulled up his shirt. Parker felt all the hands drop away instantly and his shirt fell again like a veil over the face. There was a silence in the pool room which seemed to Parker to grow from the circle around him until it extended to the foundations under the building and upward through the beams of the roof.
> Finally some one said, "Christ!" Then they all broke into noise at once. Parker turned around, an uncertain grin on his face. (526)

La scène fait pendant à celle de la révélation devant l'arbre en feu, mais cette fois c'est Parker qui est au centre et les autres qui font cercle autour de lui. Leur réaction est également celle de la stupéfaction et lorsque l'un d'entre eux s'écrit : « Christ ! », on comprend que cette fois encore l'exclamation doit être prise littéralement. L'homme vient de voir l'image du Christ, mais instinctivement il sait aussi qu'il vient de voir *sur* Parker et *en* Parker le Christ lui-même, puisque tout homme est un centre divin. O. E. Parker aura été à son tour l'agent d'une révélation. Et si, par la suite, l'image ne produit pas le même effet sur sa femme, c'est parce que le dogme de sa religion puritaine, qui lui a inculqué que toute représentation de Dieu était un péché, l'a enfermée dans un carcan trop étroit et l'empêche de voir par ses propres yeux. Elle qui croit être sauvée est encore très loin de la Vérité.

La métaphore, chez O'Connor, est le mode de fonctionnement de ceux qui ont vu la lumière car ils superposent en permanence deux images (l'une littérale et l'autre symbolique) et leur double vision s'inscrit dans un processus d'ascendance qui les mènent vers la révélation de l'union en Dieu.

Métonymie

Si la métaphore est la figure de style de l'union, la métonymie est celle de la division et du cloisonnement. Elle opère donc de préférence au niveau du littéral. C'est un moyen souvent utilisé pour caricaturer, forcer le trait et c'est donc la figure de style qui convient le mieux à la satire.

Lorsque Flannery O'Connor veut renvoyer dos à dos les mécréants et les chrétiens trop étriqués, les matérialistes et les fous de Dieu, les intellectuels et les bouseux du Sud profond, elle s'empare d'un détail de leur personne ou de leur comportement qu'elle grossit à la loupe, mais sans pour autant les déshumaniser. Au contraire, cet éclairage sur un aspect intime a pour avantage de les rendre plus proches et plus familiers. Et de montrer aussi le fonctionnement de leurs âmes.

Les détails physiques utilisés pour caractériser un personnage sont de deux ordres : le manque ou l'excès. En ce qui concerne le manque, il s'agit souvent d'un membre amputé ou atrophié (le bras de Mr. Shiftlet, la jambe de Joy/Hulga, le pied bot de Rufus Johnson, l'ulcère à la jambe de Mr. Turpin), d'une déficience mentale et/ou physique (le retard de développement de Lucynell Crater ainsi que son mutisme et sa surdité, la fièvre d'Asbury Fox, la dépendance sénile de Dudley et de Tanner, la paralysie du Général, la maladie de cœur de Joy/Hulga, la tension de Mrs. Chestny et tous les cas de myopie qui nécessitent le port de lunettes). Du côté de l'excès, on trouve beaucoup de personnages dont le poids rend la locomotion difficile (Ruby, Red Sam et Bobby Lee, Mrs. Pritchard, Mrs. Shortley, Alonzo, Mrs. Freeman, Mrs. Greenleaf, Mrs. Chestny, Mrs. Turpin). Dans cette catégorie, on peut sans doute aussi ranger l'hermaphrodite et ses deux sexes qu'il/elle exhibe dans les foires. Tous font de leur handicap une caractéristique qu'ils chérissent comme Joy/Hulga sa jambe de bois et Rufus sa chaussure orthopédique ou qu'ils cultivent comme Asbury sa maladie. C'est la marque qui les différencie, qui leur tient parfois lieu de personnalité ou qu'ils compensent par des activités de l'esprit. C'est aussi autour de cette caractéristique physique que l'intrigue va se nouer ou se dénouer et que l'action va se cristalliser (le vol de la jambe de bois, l'annonce finale que la maladie d'Asbury n'est pas incurable, l'enlèvement et l'abandon de Lucynell Crater, la crise cardiaque de Mrs. Shortley et de Mr. Fortune, l'attaque de Mrs. Chestny). Et lorsque les personnages ne souffrent pas eux-mêmes de maladies, il leur arrive de se complaire en longues litanies sur la misère humaine, comme Mrs Freeman dans « Good Country People » :

> Mrs. Freeman had a special fondness for the details of secret infections, hidden deformities, assaults upon children. Of diseases, she preferred the lingering or incurable. (275)

Certains, comme Manley Pointer, par une sorte de fétichisme pervers, vont jusqu'à collectionner les prothèses des femmes handicapées qu'ils séduisent. Et la description du magasin d'appareils orthopédiques de « The Lame Shall Enter First » tient à la fois du cabinet de curiosités et de la chambre de torture. Ces excès ont fait classer l'œuvre de Flannery O'Connor dans la catégorie du grotesque, mais on pourrait aussi bien ajouter celle du sado-masochisme dont ces personnages semblent tous souffrir peu ou prou. Car leur cruauté mentale n'est pas moindre que leur capacité à endurer la souffrance physique.

La métonymie ne fonctionne pas seulement à partir de caractéristiques physiques. Certains objets ou articles de vêtements reviennent souvent dans les différents récits. Les valises mystérieuses des personnages d'intrus peuvent apparaître dans un premier temps comme des garanties de sérieux, mais elles se révèlent souvent être des leurres. Le vêtement sert en général à définir la classe sociale, bien que certains jeunes gens se plaisent à brouiller les pistes. Julian, par exemple, lorsqu'il accompagne sa mère qui veut prendre l'autobus, enlève sa cravate, ce que la vieille dame trouve tout à fait insupportable, et, lorsque, cédant à son insistance, il la remet, ce ne peut être qu'avec la remarque ironique : « Restored to my class » (409). Joy/Hulga, elle aussi, s'ingénie à choquer sa mère, d'abord en changeant de prénom et en choisissant le plus hideux qu'elle ait pu trouver, puis en s'habillant dans des tenues délibérément ridicules :

> Here she went about all day in a six-year-old skirt and a yellow sweat shirt with a faded cowboy on a horse embossed on it. She thought it was funny; Mrs. Hopewell thought it was idiotic and showed simply that she was still a child She was brilliant but she didn't have a grain of sense. (276)

Un certain nombre de chapeaux, dans les nouvelles, sont également ridicules. Mais, outre cette caractéristique, celui de Mrs. Chestny est aussi un ressort de l'intrigue puisqu'il va lui faire rencontrer « son double noir », ce qui aura une conséquence fatale pour elle. Non pas que la vue du couvre-chef semblable au sien déclenche la colère de la femme noire, mais cette ressemblance laisse supposer que la femme partage d'autres traits de caractère avec Mrs. Chestny, en particulier l'orgueil et l'obstination, et l'on n'est pas surpris qu'elle réagisse violemment devant une humiliation. Le coup de poing qu'elle assène à Mrs. Chestny est une manifestation bien ironique de la convergence prônée par le titre de la nouvelle !

Parmi les articles de vêtements, il faut faire une place particulière au traitement des chaussures chez Flannery O'Connor. Dans les lieux publics, comme l'autobus ou la salle d'attente du médecin, les chaussures, plus que tout autre chose, servent à établir une hiérarchie entre les personnages. Dans « Revelation », Mrs Turpin, qui focalise le récit, « always noticed people's feet » (490) :

> The well-dressed lady had on red and gray suede shoes to match her dress. Mrs. Turpin had on her good black patent leather pumps. The ugly girl had on Girl Scout shoes and heavy socks. The old woman had on tennis shoes and the white-trashy mother had on what appeared to be bedroom slippers, black straw with gold braid threaded through them – exactly what you would have expected her to have on. [...] Next to the child's mother was a red-headed youngish woman, reading one of the magazines and working a piece of chewing gum [...] Mrs Turpin could not see the woman's feet. She was not white-trash, just common. (491)

Lorsque la jeune femme dont Mrs. Turpin ne pouvait pas voir les pieds passe devant elle pour entrer dans le cabinet du médecin, on peut voir, grâce à une seule phrase courte et sans commentaire, que le jugement de Mrs. Turpin, qui l'avait classée comme vulgaire, était infaillible : « She had on red high-heeled shoes » (493) !

Dans « Everything that Rises Must Converge », Mrs. Chestny accorde également une grande importance aux chaussures des passagers du bus. Et, dans cette nouvelle, on voit que les distinctions qu'elle établit entre les gens s'articulent en outre sur une dialectique « être »/« avoir ». Au début du récit, Mrs. Chestny répète à son fils qu'en dépit de ses revers de fortune, sa place dans le monde n'a pas changé. Devant l'air sceptique de Julian, elle décline sous différentes formes la phrase suivante : « I know who I am » (407). En particulier, elle lui explique : « You remain what you are, » she said, « Your great-grandfather had a plantation and two hundred slaves. » (408). Où l'on voit que "what you are" dépend étroitement de "what you have" ou, à défaut, "had". Et, dans le cas de Mrs. Chestny, cette identité est plus particulièrement liée au fait que ses ancêtres aient possédé des esclaves. Dans l'autobus, la dialectique être/avoir revient sous une autre forme. La ségrégation dans les lieux publics étant à présent interdite, la mère de Julian redoute d'y côtoyer des Noirs et, lorsqu'elle s'est assurée que le bus n'en contenait pas, elle lance à la cantonade : « I see we have the bus to ourselves » (410). « We have » et « ourselves » incluent tous les Blancs qui se trouvent à cet instant dans cet autobus. Or, en face d'elle, est assise une femme qui a été identifiée, de manière métonymique, par ses pieds maigres chaussés de « red and white canvas sandals » (410). Des sandales de toile ne vous classent pas dans la même catégorie que des chaussures de cuir. Il y a donc tout à parier que la femme en question est quelqu'un que Mrs. Chestny qualifierait habituellement de « white trash ». Mais, ce jour-là, elle se doit de l'inclure dans le groupe des « ourselves ». Or, puisque seuls les possédants sont respectables, la femme, lorsqu'elle est mentionnée à nouveau, devient : « *the owner* of the red and white canvas sandals » (410, c'est moi qui souligne). Si l'on articule cette obsession de la possession avec le souvenir de l'esclavage, on comprend mieux pourquoi celle-ci est indissociable de l'identité. En effet, dans le Sud esclavagiste, « to have » voulait dire posséder des biens mais aussi des êtres humains. Et ceux qui ne possédaient pas, *étaient possédés*, c'est-à-dire qu'ils n'étaient rien. Dans cette perspective, le fait que « to be » soit lié à « to have » prend donc un relief particulier.

Au-delà de ces considérations socio-historiques, la métonymie, dans les nouvelles de Flannery O'Connor, renvoie à la vision parcellaire que les personnages ont du monde, eux qui vivent des existences divisées dans des espaces confinés. Cette perception étroite et réduite des choses est figurée par les nombreux cadres (fenêtres, portes, vitres de voitures, lunettes) qui limitent la vue et bornent l'horizon des protagonistes. L'un des exemples les plus frappants est sans doute celui de l'enfant de « A Circle in the Fire » qui ne voit que les jambes de sa mère et de Mrs. Pritchard en se penchant par-dessus la rampe du premier étage (« Mrs. Cope's and Mrs. Pritchard's legs were facing each other in the hall », 181). À cela, il faut ajouter tous les exemples de personnages qui se cachent pour en épier d'autres sans être vus. On citera Thomas, entre le mur et le rideau de sa chambre, regardant l'arrivée de Sarah Ham et de sa mère ; les Noirs, cachés derrière un buisson, pour voir « The Displaced Person », puis Mrs. Shortley les observant par-derrière avant d'aller espionner un moment son mari ; plus tard, la même Mrs. Shortley écoutera depuis une remise la conversation du prêtre et de Mrs. McIntyre où elle apprendra que son mari va bientôt être renvoyé ; la fillette de « A Temple of the Holy Ghost » grimpe sur un tonneau pour ne pas perdre une miette de ce que se disent les deux filles et les deux garçons sur la véranda ; Mr. Fortune se dissimule derrière un arbre pour voir Pitts fouetter sa fille, punition que Mary accepte pour maintenir l'équilibre des pouvoirs entre les deux hommes, mais nie farouchement avoir reçue lorsqu'il lui en parle ; Julian et son voisin noir se retranchent derrière un journal dans le bus et ne parviennent pas à communiquer ; Norton se cache dans le placard à vêtements de sa mère pour échapper à l'emprise de Rufus ; Dudley observe les allées et venues du voisin noir sur le palier de l'immeuble. Et cette liste n'est bien évidemment pas exhaustive.

Outre ceux qui cherchent à voir sans être vus, il y a aussi un nombre très important de personnages qui ne parviennent pas à fixer leur regard sur leur interlocuteur et pratiquent une vision de côté, de biais, ou « à la périphérie d'un cercle », comme Mr. Greenleaf. Ou ceux, non moins nombreux (au moins un dans chaque nouvelle) qui s'efforcent d'être « expressionless », de ne pas manifester d'émotions ou de sentiments, de rendre leur visage impénétrable. Autant de stratégies d'isolement volontaire qui font de leur corps une prison dont seul un choc violent pourra les délivrer.

Conclusion : « As if… »

Toute l'œuvre de Flannery O'Connor pourrait tenir dans un « as if », inscrivant dans ses textes une position liminale, un entre-deux vacillant, instable, fluctuant, à l'interface entre une réalité décevante, peuplée d'êtres médiocres aux limitations trop humaines, et un au-delà mystérieux aussi désirable qu'inatteignable. Le point d'équilibre entre ces extrêmes n'est jamais trouvé. Et il n'est sans doute pas même souhaité puisque seule la violence produit le choc nécessaire à l'éveil des consciences endormies.

« As if » est une forme grammaticale récurrente dans les contes de Poe que nous avons cités aux chapitres 8 et 9. Ils y introduisent l'impossibilité de dire le sens avec certitude, ou plutôt la conviction que les sens ne sont pas suffisants à rendre compte des mystères du monde. Chez le maître du conte fantastique, il s'agit de folie, d'hallucinations, de perceptions déréglées. Avec la conviction, toujours, que le mal est partout et que la mort rôde. Les mêmes obsessions hantent la prose d'O'Connor avec toutefois, au bout, un espoir de salut. Un espoir, une foi, chevillés au corps, « comme si » on ne savait pas, comme si on faisait semblant d'ignorer que les mots tracés sur la page ne perdent jamais de leur opacité. Comme si le sens ne pouvait pas bifurquer à chaque détour de syllabes, à chaque nouveau mot qui s'en va batailler contre les autres ou qui échoue en piles comme ces corps fragmentés qui se sont imprimés dans un coin du cerveau de Mrs. Shortley sans qu'elle sache pourquoi :

> She began to imagine a war of words coming at each other, to see the Polish words and the English words coming at each other, stalking forward, not sentences, just words, gabble gabble gabble, flung out high and shrill and stalking forward and then grappling with each other. She saw the Polish words, dirty and all-knowing and unreformed, flinging mud on the clean English words until everything was equally dirty. She saw them all piled up

> in a room, all the dead dirty words, theirs and hers too, piled up like the naked bodies in the newsreel. *God save me, she cried silently, from the stinking power of Satan!* (209, c'est moi qui souligne)

« God », « Satan », les voilà bien les deux mots, retranchés à chaque bout de la phrase, prêts à se livrer une guerre sans merci, par-dessus d'autres mots qui ont aussi tiré leurs épées : save/power ; cried/ silently – batailles d'oxymores entre qui aucun pouce de terrain ne sera jamais lâché, à moins que ces mots ne soient au fond d'accord sur une chose : barricader les entrées, ne rien laisser passer, faire semblant de dire et laisser planer – encore et toujours – le doute.

Bibliographie

Asals, Frederick. *Flannery O'Connor: The Imagination of Extremity.* Athens: The University of Georgia Press, 1982.

Benet's Reader's *Encyclopedia of American Literature.* Glasgow: Harper Collins, 1992.

Brisac, Geneviève. *Loin du Paradis. Flannery O'Connor.* Paris : Edition de l'Olivier, 1991.

Bleikasten, André. *Flannery O'Connor. In Extremis.* Paris : Belin, 2004.

Daleux, André. *Teilhard de Chardin : Science et foi réconciliées ?* Paris : Ed. Gabriandre, 2001.

Delta. Flannery O'Connor et le réalisme des lointains. Montpellier : Université Paul Valéry, 1976 (excellentes études, près du texte, contrairement à la plupart des études américaines qui traitent surtout de la thématique religieuse).

Desmond, John F. *Risen Sons: Flannery O'Connor's Vision of History.* Athens: The University of Georgia Press, 1987. (Some good passages, but a lot of theological considerations and a lot of repetitions)

Dictionnaire de la Théologie chrétienne. Encyclopaedia Universalis. Paris : Albin Michel, 1998.

Di Renzo, Anthony. *American Gargoyles: Flannery O'Connor and the Medieval Grotesque.* Carbondale: Southern Illinois University Press, 1993.

Dommergues, Pierre. *L'aliénation dans le roman américain contemporain.* Paris : 10/18, 1977. Chapitre VII, de 7 à 64, sur Flannery O'Connor.

Duperray, Annick (dir.). *The Complete Stories, Flannery O'Connor.* Paris : Ellipses, 2004.

Eggenschwiler, David. *The Christian Humanism of Flannery O'Connor.* Detroit: Wayne State University Press, 1972. (Good exploration of the problem of evil, notably.)

Ellsberg, Robert. *Flannery O'Connor: Spiritual Writings.* Maryknoll, NY: Orbis Books, 2003.

Friedman, Melvin J. and Lawson, Lewis A. *The Added Dimension: The Art and Mind of Flannery O'Connor.* New York: Fordham University Press, 1966. Reprint 1989. (Very good essays.)

Gentry, Bruce. *Flannery O'Connor's Religion of the Grotesque.* Jackson: University of Mississippi Press, 1986.

Gordon, Sarah. *Flannery O'Connor: The Obedient Imagination.* Athens: The University of Georgia Press, 2000.

Hardy, Donald E. *Narrating Knowledge in Flannery O'Connor.* Columbia, SC: University of South Carolina Press, 2003.

HENDIN, Josephine. *The World of Flannery O'Connor.* Bloomington: Indiana University Press, 1970)

HYMAN, Stanley Edgar. *Flannery O'Connor*. Minneapolis: University of Minnesota, 1966. (A good and short introduction to her work.)

KILCOURSE, George A. *Flannery O'Connor's Religious Imagination.* New York, Mahwah, NJ: Paulist Press, 2001.

MAGEE, Rosemary. *Conversations with Flannery O'Connor.* Jackson: University of Mississippi Press, 1987.

MARTIN, Regis. *Unmasking the Devil: Dramas of Sin and Grace in the World of Flannery O'Connor.* Ypsilanti, MI: Sapientia Press, 2002.

MURPHY, John J. *Flannery O'Connor and the Christian Mystery.* Provo: Brigham Young University, 1997.

O'CONNOR, Flannery. *The Complete Stories*. Edition used: London: Faber and Faber, 1990.

— *Mystery and Manners.* Sally and Robert Fizgerald, eds. New York: Farrar, Straus and Giroux, 1969.

— *The Habit of Being*, S. Fitzgerald, ed. New York: Farrar and Strauss, 1979.

ORWELL, Miles. *Invisible Parade: The Fiction of Flannery O'Connor.* Philadelphia: Temple University Press, 1972. Reprinted under the title: *Flannery O'Connor: An Introduction.* (Good essays).

PERRIN-CHENOUR, Marie-Claude (dir.). *The Complete Stories, Flannery O'Connor.* Paris : Éditions du Temps, 2004.

POTHIER, Jacques. *Les nouvelles de Flannery O'Connor.* Nantes : Éditions de l'Université de Versailles Saint-Quentin-en-Yvelines, 2004.

PROWN, Katherine Hemple. *Revising Flannery O'Connor: Southern Literary Culture and the Problem of Female Authorship.* Charlottesville: University Press of Virginia, 2001.

RATH, Sura P. & SHAW Mary Neff. *Flannery O'Connor: New Perspectives.* Athens: The University of Georgia Press, 1996.

RICHARD, Claude. "Désir et destin in 'A Good Man Is Hard to Find'". *Delta* n° 2, mars 1976, 61-73.

ROUGÉ, Robert. *L'inquiétude religieuse dans le roman américain.* Thèse, vers 1975. (Une grande partie porte sur Flannery O'Connor.)

SINGLETON, Charles S. *Dante's Commedia : Elements of Structure.* (1954) Baltimore: John Hopkins UP, 1977.

STEPHENS, Martha. *The Question of Flannery O'Connor.* Baton Rouge: The University of Louisiana Press, 1973.

TEILHARD DE CHARDIN, Pierre. *Le Milieu divin*, Paris : Seuil, 1957.

WESTARP, Karl Heinz. Precision and Depth in *Flannery O'Connor's Short Stories.* Aarhus: Aarhus University Press, 2002.

WHITT, Margaret Early. *Understanding Flannery O'Connor.* Columbia, SC: University of South Carolina Press, 1997.

WOOD, Ralph C. *Flannery O'Connor and the Christ-Haunted South.* Grand Rapid, Michigan: William B. Eerdmans Publishing Company, 2004. (Passionnantes analyses du rapport entre le catholicisme et le protestantisme du Sud.)

Armand Colin Éditeur
21, rue du Montparnasse, 75006 Paris
10116343 - (I) - (3,2) - OSB 100° - NOC - ODS
Dépôt légal : décembre 2004

Achevé d'imprimer sur les presses de
SNEL Grafics sa
rue Saint-Vincent 12 – B-4020 Liège
Tél +32(0)4 344 65 60 - Fax +32(0)4 341 48 41
décembre 2004 — 33626

Imprimé en Belgique